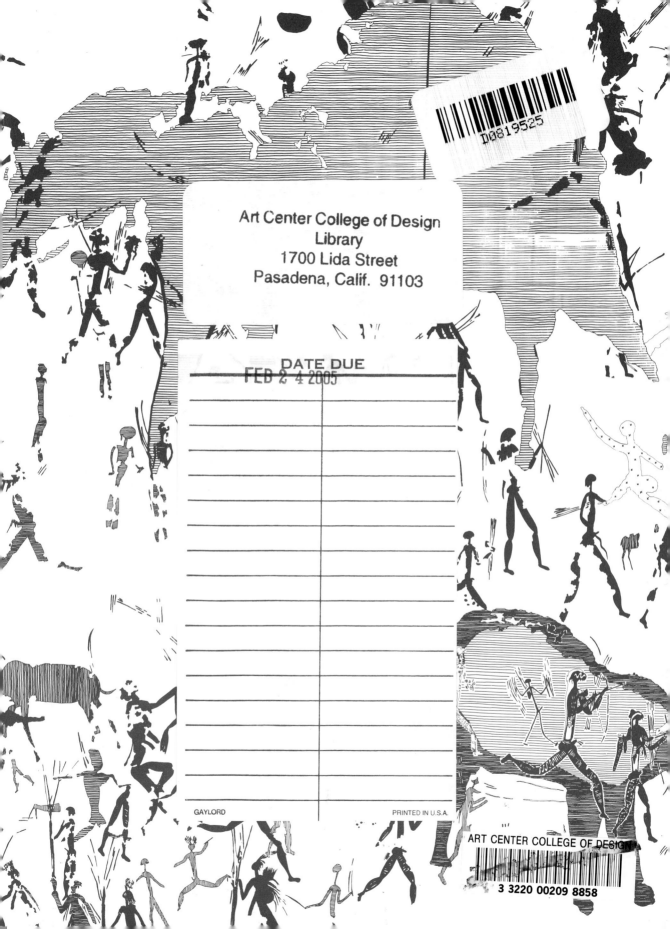

THE HUNTER'S VISION

THE HUNTER'S VISION

THE PREHISTORIC ART OF ZIMBABWE

Peter Garlake

BRITISH MUSEUM PRESS

© 1995 Peter Garlake

Published by British Museum Press
A division of British Museum Publications Ltd
46 Bloomsbury Street
London WC1B 3QQ

ISBN 0–7141–2518–0

British Library Cataloguing in Publication data is available

Designed by Behram Kapadia

Typeset by Create Publishing Services
Printed and bound in Great Britain by
The Bath Press, Avon.

NOTE ON THE ILLUSTRATIONS

The scale on many of the illustrations is shown by a
circle: the diameter of a quartered circle
indicates 2 cm, that of a plain circle 1 cm.

ENDPAPERS *Part of the paintings in
one of the larger caves. The frieze is
over 17.5 m long and over 5 m
above ground level. Vestiges of
paint show that originally the
paintings extended down to the
ground, so only about a quarter of
them now survive. They are
reproduced about one-sixth actual
size. Bindura.*

1 *(previous page) This painting can
be interpreted as an encounter
between groups of hunters. Detailed
analysis of their accoutrements
suggests additional significance for
the composition. Makoni.*

CONTENTS

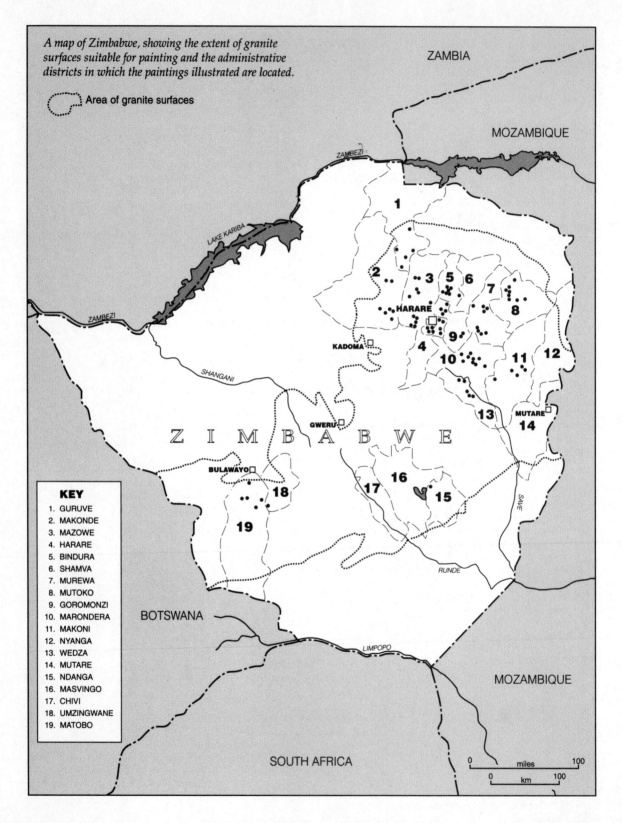

A map of Zimbabwe, showing the extent of granite surfaces suitable for painting and the administrative districts in which the paintings illustrated are located.

⋯⋯⋯⋯ Area of granite surfaces

ZAMBIA

MOZAMBIQUE

ZAMBEZI

LAKE KARIBA

ZAMBEZI

SHANGANI

1

2

3 5 6

HARARE

7

8

KADOMA

4

9

10

11 12

13

MUTARE

14

Z I M B A B W E

GWERU

BULAWAYO

18

16

17 15

19

SAVE

RUNDE

BOTSWANA

LIMPOPO

MOZAMBIQUE

SOUTH AFRICA

KEY
1. GURUVE
2. MAKONDE
3. MAZOWE
4. HARARE
5. BINDURA
6. SHAMVA
7. MUREWA
8. MUTOKO
9. GOROMONZI
10. MARONDERA
11. MAKONI
12. NYANGA
13. WEDZA
14. MUTARE
15. NDANGA
16. MASVINGO
17. CHIVI
18. UMZINGWANE
19. MATOBO

0 ___ miles ___ 100

0 ___ km ___ 100

PREFACE

This book is about one of the world's last and greatest undiscovered artistic and cultural treasures: the prehistoric paintings of Zimbabwe. There are many thousands of sites with paintings in the granite hills, caves and shelters and under the overhangs of many scattered boulders in Zimbabwe, most of them still unrecorded. They were created many hundreds and, in some cases, thousands of years ago. They are so old that the societies that created them disappeared entirely so long ago that they are absent not just from the region's short recorded history but, except in the most shadowy and fragmentary form, from folk memory as well.

The central issue of any discussion or study of the paintings is the question of whether they should be considered true or valid 'art'. Are they simply childish or primitive attempts to reproduce things seen, superficial attempts to record the trivia of everyday life, and thus no more than doodles or graffiti? If they are this banal, they can be of little interest except perhaps to archaeologists attempting to reconstruct material aspects of prehistoric life. Or are they deeply rooted in the perceptions, beliefs, metaphysics and spirit of their vanished culture? If they are, their study must be one of consuming interest to a much greater range of people. The definitions of art are infinite and this is no place to explore them. Rather, I will quote, almost at random, two descriptions of art that I came across while I was writing this preface, one by a leading critic of modern art and the other by a leading art historian concerned with traditional African art. 'The discipline of art [is] indicated by a love of structure, clarity, complexity, nuance and imaginative ambition.' 'The power that I attribute to

2 *The kudu antelope is the commonest animal painted. The horns and hair of this bull have been greatly exaggerated, perhaps to emphasise its masculinity. Marondera.*

3 *Plants were regularly if not frequently depicted but are seldom identifiable. The hunters have been given bows of an impossible size. Mutoko.*

art [is] the power to transform, to create new realities, to offer new possibilities, to create responses, to confound, and to do things that otherwise cannot be done.'[1] On such criteria or on any others that could have been chosen, I have no doubt that the prehistoric paintings of Zimbabwe qualify as art. I believe, on the evidence of the paintings themselves, that they are an expression of a true artistic tradition, indeed a highly sophisticated and important one. In the end, this is what I seek to justify in my work. This book is an exploration of the visual, cultural, intellectual, emotional and spiritual richness and complexity of a hitherto unexplored artistic tradition.

From what the paintings themselves record of their artists' societies and from analogies with much more recent San paintings in South Africa, we can be certain that the artists were San people who had a Stone Age technology and obtained their sustenance through hunting and gathering. Only pitiful, scattered, frightened and fragmented remnants of San communities survived into this century in Zimbabwe. The processes by which the San societies that once flourished throughout Zimbabwe were extinguished – through development, adaptation, absorption or by being driven from the farmlands of the highveld – have not yet been traced by prehistorians.

The San are popularly known as 'Bushmen'. As this very name makes so clear, they were a people long reviled by black and white alike: the foreigners who invaded their territories killed the game on which they depended and in the end destroyed their societies. During the last three hundred years San in South Africa were hunted down, enslaved and killed – men, women and children – in systematic campaigns of extermination as shameful as any the world has known. Genocide, as always, was justified by the persecutors by reducing their victims to sub-human status, unworthy of any consideration or respect. Before they became extinct, some San were able

4 *Sable or roan antelope lying down with, as the principles of the art demanded, their legs shown free of their bodies. Next to them is another plant form. Mazowe.*

to tell something about themselves. Others, still clinging to parts of their heritage in the Kalahari, have been sympathetically studied by anthropologists over the last forty years.[2] Through the work over the last twenty years of David Lewis-Williams in South Africa, the understanding of San beliefs had brought the paintings there back to life.[3]

For a century and more before this, the paintings had been the subject of speculation. This in no way increased understanding of the art, but simply provided insights into each researcher's own preconceptions and cultural background. It imposed a great variety of inappropriate and alien ideas about the nature of art, of artists and of artists' relationships with their societies. By the time they were adopted in southern Africa most of these ideas were already outmoded and had long been discarded as a method of dealing with the art of the countries for which they had been developed. They were clearly remote not just from the reality of the rock paintings or of the San but from all reality.

In eight years of study, I have tried in Zimbabwe to look at the paintings with the care, consideration and respect that I think they deserve. In contrast to the sweeping and unsubstantiated generalisations of so much previous work, I try to demonstrate every point I make through specific paintings which I have copied. I have attempted comparative analyses of many paintings, analyses not just of individual images, but of sets of images, of defined visual themes, and of the associations and relationships between them. The paintings are my primary source, but not the only one. I hope my interpretations are informed by some understanding, albeit second-hand, of San societies, the way they thought about and made sense of their world, their perceptions and beliefs.

This is not an account of the progress of my research; that has been given elsewhere. In *The Painted Caves*, stimulated by the current work in South Africa, I attempted to clear my mind of the irrelevant clutter of the many erroneous approaches and ideas that I and most people had accepted until then. I tried to map out what seemed to be some of the real significances of the paintings of Zimbabwe and how these could be investigated further.[4] I have given a detailed account of my subsequent research, of the arguments that led to my present interpretations in a thesis.[5] In *The Hunter's Vision*, I present a digest of my conclusions illustrated by sites and paintings, almost none of which has been published before. Because it is not primarily concerned with argument or demonstration, much of it may sound assertive or dogmatic.

It is a description of the view from the particular vantage point at which I now pause, a stage in a climb. It is not an account of the climb, still less do I claim it as a view from the summit. The climb is not over,

5 A conceptual or invented creature. The nearest painted equivalent to the shape of its tail is a fly whisk. Goromonzi.

9

nor can it ever be. Those who read it look out on the country through my eyes. My descriptions of it will be in part distorted and much is still partly or entirely obscured in shadow. But it is also, I hope, more than description. I try to interpret the underlying bedrock and the growths this encourages, the factors that helped to form the landscape we see. I draw attention to what seem to me salient features, what seem useful routes and signposts for further progress towards the unattainable summit. I have found the climb so far a marvellous experience and the glimpses it gives of the unimagined richness of the land around encourage me to try to climb higher. I hope my work will also encourage other climbers and that they will pioneer other routes leading on to other vistas.

Once again, I express my gratitude and thanks to all who have helped me in this work: the many landowners who have gone to considerable trouble to guide me to paintings on their properties; the many people living near paintings who have done the same; people who have informed me of further paintings; and those who have helped me in tracing the paintings, especially Courtney Yilk, Sophie Golay-Lescuyer, Teresa Garlake and Sasha Wales-Smith. There are a great many others who have given great help in many different ways, especially Anglo-American Corporation Services of Zimbabwe, John Picton, my wife Margaret and, in showing me many sites in the Matopo Hills, David Erwee and Elspeth Parry. Without them, there would be no book.

Paintings are very vulnerable to vandalism and damage. In the present state of the care that is given them by those responsible for their conservation in Zimbabwe, secrecy is their best protection. Many have asked that I do not reveal the locations of paintings they have shown me. This I respect. All names and places are omitted here. This does not seem to me to matter greatly: the paintings discussed and illustrated are intended as representative samples and what I say about them applies to a range of similar paintings.

Borrowdale Homestead,
Harare, August 1993

INTRODUCTION

Paintings are to be found wherever granites outcrop on the surface of the highveld plateau of the tropical African interior between the Zambezi and Limpopo river valleys. The paintings and the granites are inextricably linked. The granite hills provided shelter for the paintings, the artists and their communities. Granite soils and bedrock determine the vegetation and fauna of the region as well as affording vantage points from which hunters saw their game, the animals they painted. Granite is the setting for the paintings and the surface for which they were designed. The rocks form a unique landscape of immense antiquity which for many has an unmatched beauty and enchantment. Granite is a symbol of endurance and immutability; yet here, under a bleaching sun and exposed in season to violent storms, these ancient rocks have been cracked, stained and eroded by water and weather into strange patterns and shapes. Great cliff-girt masses seem elephantine in size, colour and texture, appearing unalterable yet worn, their heights revealing sponges of grass and soil enough for a few hardy trees and ancient pools of fresh water from which tiny trickles have cut channels deep into the rock surfaces. The flanks of many hills are hollowed into great open caves, always in deep, cool shadow.

The granites of Zimbabwe are extremely hard and ancient rocks. Millions of years ago they rose in liquid form from the earth's centre and cooled and solidified far beneath the earth's surface. They have only been exposed through aeons of erosion of the softer soils and rocks that once covered them. As the bubbles of liquid granite cooled, they developed lines of stress and as the exposed granite weathered

6 *The exfoliated remains of a warthog superimposed on a hunter. His head is conceived as two elements: a bossed forehead and a protruding jaw, a regular convention of the art. Murewa.*

7 *A large fish and a vivid little image of a man attacking a small antelope. Bindura.*

slowly on the earth's surface through the action of daily and seasonal temperature changes, expansion and contraction, it split and cracked along these lines of stress. Where the stress lines formed a grid of horizontal and vertical lines, the granite mass weathered to form the 'castle kopjes' and 'balancing rocks' that are such a feature of Zimbabwe's skylines. Boulders are sculpted to improbable shapes and piled one on another in absurd instability, deep tunnels leading between them. Elsewhere, the stresslines followed the surfaces of the original granite globules, and their exposed surfaces peeled away like an 'onion's skin' producing great bare 'domes' and 'whale backs'. Where there were fast-weathering inclusions in the granite, decay and flaking centred round these and gradually increased and enlarged to produce smooth, rounded, domed hollows, great caves within the granite mass.

A single bolt of lightning on water-soaked rock can bring tens of thousands of tons of stone crashing down the slopes of a granite dome. Fire can have a devastating and terrible effect on exposed granite, causing the entire surface to split, exfoliate and fall as thin, irregular slivers or spalls. Water running over a surface even as hard and impervious as granite will gradually dissolve salts in the rock, bring these to the surface, deposit them as it evaporates and stain the rock in every shade of pink, yellow and white. It can form transparent, translucent or opaque films over the surface and over paintings on it, sometimes helping to preserve them, sometimes partly or entirely obscuring them.

The coarse sand soils of the granite do not encourage dense vegetation and though they are easily tilled, they are far from ideal for continuous farming. If they are left undisturbed, the abundant water from the hills nourishes woodland of tall trees. The granite cliffs are still home to nesting eagles and a host of lesser birds. Busy and inquisitive rock rabbits inhabit every crevice; baboons make the rocks echo with their barking challenges. Small antelope specially adapted to life in the hills can still sometimes be seen, as can pythons and other

8 *Complex and unnatural patterning on fish: red dots on white stripes alternate with white dots on unpainted stripes. The significance of such dots is explored in Chapter 5. Guruve.*

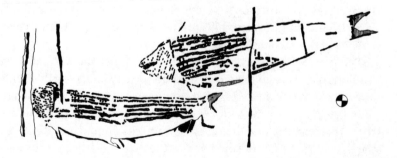

9 *A snake, probably a python, covered with careful lines of dots, a pattern that has no correspondence with the visible world. Mutoko.*

snakes that seek the warmth of sun-drenched surfaces. Before the heat of full day brings rest, some hills are still alive with the noise of wild life. Below, the plains seem now to lie silent and lifeless, denuded, divided into small holdings and dotted with villages and people working their fields. But even within the last hundred years they were home to some of the richest herds of game, in variety and numbers, that the world has seen. Little more than a century ago, hunters could describe river banks black for many miles with herds of elephant and buffalo, or plains covered with herds of every variety of antelope, zebra, wildebeeste, giraffe and ostrich, all easily visible from a single vantage point.

This abundance of life is now only preserved in the paintings, which occur everywhere among the hills and on the boulders of the plain. They are small, fragile, often faint and fragmentary, but equally often seeming as fresh as the day the artist drew his last brush stroke, the marks of its hairs still visible across the surface. They are concealed, undocumented, unprotected, indeed many are so unvisited and ignored that it seems as if no one has seen them since the last artist wandered away. Few local people today recognise any merit in these paintings; they are seen as the work of ghosts, marking places where spirits and ancestors wander. Many visitors consider them the scribblings of superstitious savages, unable and unfit to survive and rightly swept aside by the onward march of evolutionary progress. Their paintings are too simple, crude and impoverished to have anything to say or to be of any interest.

Certainly the paintings are the opposite of the great monuments of civilisations. They do not proclaim themselves with the bombast of majesty or military might, soar with the aspirations of temples, churches and cathedrals, or cloak death with the vanity of tombs. They have to be laboriously searched out; each discovery is unexpected and exciting. They are the work of people whose culture

10 *Three hunters whose bodies were originally covered with white stripes. Murewa.*

13

11 In the last of a long sequence of paintings, the outline of an elephant was superimposed on a composition made up of ovoid shapes in different colours, which were frequently renewed and extended as the panel of paintings was enlarged. The human figures along the top and at the right are particularly strange and striking. Wedza.

and way of life and whose perceptions of their world and the beliefs they developed to make sense of these, are entirely alien to us.

One of the most appealing qualities of the paintings is the fact that they still exist in the places where they were painted. However much of the country round them and its human and animal populations may have changed, the physical context is still essentially the same as it was when the artists were at work. They sat on the same stones, balanced on the same rocks as they painted, worked in the same light, and looked out over the same stunning views when they had finished. Unlike the art of almost every other culture, these paintings cannot be removed to galleries and museums, be given a price tag or become subject to the changing fashions of display. They cannot even be reproduced in the fullness of their colour or texture. Even the most

12 *A typical panel of disparate images. At the top is a group of hunters set next to a composition of oval shapes. Below there are fish, a baby rhino, a zebra with its head lowered and bleeding and further rhino. Goromonzi.*

meticulous copies in oil or watercolour on paper lose all veracity through using media and surfaces so different from those of the artists. Photographs give only very broad and general impressions of character at the expense of detail. Tracings and copies in black and white can bring out detail with clarity and serve many useful purposes but are more diagrams than facsimiles. Nothing can match the originals in their impact. This is art in the places for which it was created. And to experience it one must expend considerable time and effort, undergo the prolonged anticipation, the climbs and searches through shadowed woods and up slippery rock-strewn slopes, in fact share in the pilgrimage of the artists. This is an integral part of the experience of rock paintings.

Dating

The rock paintings of southern Africa have not yet been dated directly, because the paints that were used do not contain the organic materials in the quantities at present required for radiocarbon or other similar dating methods. Some form of painting almost certainly took place throughout the long prehistory of Zimbabwe: pieces of the pigments identical to those used in the rock paintings have been found, rubbed and scratched through human use, in even the earliest undisturbed archaeological deposits. These were not necessarily used for painting or drawing on the rock surfaces; they could have been used for decorating anything from clothes to the body itself. Even if they were used for painting the walls of rock shelters, the paintings must have been weathered away in remote antiquity and we can have no idea what they may have been like.

The best evidence for the date of the surviving paintings comes from excavations in painted caves and shelters of the Matopo Hills in western Zimbabwe by the archaeologist Nicholas Walker.[6] He recovered scores of small spalls of granite that had traces of paintings on them. They had exfoliated from the painted granite surfaces above his excavations and been incorporated in sealed layers of Later Stone Age occupation deposits. These deposits could be dated from charcoal fragments that were also incorporated in them. The dates ranged from 13000 to 5000 years ago. Further, one of the sites with paintings had been virtually abandoned as early as 8500 years ago. Even more surprisingly, a cave with the most technically and artistically complex of all the paintings in Zimbabwe last saw any substantial occupation some 6000 years ago. These dates suggest that the art is a great deal older than previous authorities had assumed. The main argument against any great antiquity for the paintings has been that

13 *Hunters shoot a zebra. It is surrounded by unintelligible signs, the large dots perhaps signifying blood. Unintentionally, the zebra calf next to it was not completed: two legs still had to be added. Bindura.*

granite weathers and exfoliates too rapidly for paintings to survive more than a few centuries at most. From an analysis of the quantities of spalls in his excavations, Walker calculated that in fact granite flakes off at very variable rates, depending in part on how protected it is from exposure to temperature and weather changes. Exfoliation is a random occurrence and can be very rare, taking place on average perhaps only once in 8000 to 10000 years.

Furthermore, there is the evidence of the paintings themselves. Their commonest subject is men armed with bows and arrows, the characteristic weapons of the Later Stone Age. A very few depict domesticated sheep, animals first introduced to Zimbabwe and herded by a few Later Stone Age communities, probably not much more than 2500 years ago. There are no paintings to suggest that the painters had any knowledge of agriculture, crops, farm implements, pottery, metalwork, villages or any domesticated animals but sheep and dogs. All the evidence of the paintings themselves thus confirms that they are at least 1000 years old, because by this time farming was well established and widespread throughout the granite country. It also suggests that they are probably over 2000 years old, the date at which the changes associated with farming began to affect the region.

Techniques

A fresh, unweathered granite surface is far from uniform; it sparkles with many grains of different minerals and various inclusions of other rocks, including long veins of hard white quartz. Artists chose a working surface with some care. Paintings now survive mainly on surfaces protected from sun and rain, but this could be the result of selective preservation and perhaps they were once a great deal more widespread. One surface that seems to have been particularly favoured was that exposed when the bottom portion of a large boulder had split along horizontal and vertical fracture planes and fallen away from the main mass. This provided a fresh, smooth, vertical surface protected by a horizontal overhang on the parent boulder. Artists seldom took any account of the textures or even extreme changes in the colours of the rock which they were painting. They painted over water stains and across fresh exfoliation scars and generally ignored humps or hollows, impurities or chance shapes created by changes in colour or texture: the sorts of things that reminded artists in other traditions of subjects and they embellished so that the irregularities have been incorporated in their compositions. Some authorities claim to have seen evidence that some artists prepared their surfaces by rubbing them smooth or covering them with a clear varnish before they began to paint. I have not been able to distinguish such preparation anywhere.

For pigments, the artists dug out nodules of various ironstones or iron oxides – such as haematite and magnetite – from some of the hills bordering the granite. These they pounded, crushed and rubbed to a very fine powder, using pestles and mortars of harder coarser rocks like granite, which have been found in excavations. Iron oxides gave colours in every shade from the darkest reds to browns, ochres and yellows. Fire can change their colours but, being mineral or earth pigments, they do not fade at all, unlike organic colours or dyes made from plants. Hence the remarkable preservation of paintings over very long spans of time. White pigment was made from kaolin clays or by crushing quartz; the powder was not as fine or smooth as the others so it did not stick to rock surfaces as well or last as long as the other pigments.

Artists carefully mixed their powdered pigments with a binding medium on stone palettes, which have also been found in excavations. Historical records and experiments in South Africa suggest that binding agents included animal fats and blood or components of blood treated in various ways. They chose their media to ensure that they produced a paint that did not discolour, remained dense, opaque and also fluid, was easily manipulated, stuck to the rock

14 *Two very young tsessebe, one walking on still unsteady legs. An aproned woman, her body formed in rounded curves, touches the head of an attenuated figure with a horned head, painted in a very different 'style'. Guruve.*

15 *A large painting of a young antelope in which the painted infill was not completed. Bindura.*

16 *An elephant cow protects her calf. Hands have had designs painted on them and then been pressed against the rock. Bindura.*

surface well and then dried rapidly yet did not crack or flake away from the surface. Paints were thick, opaque and uniform in colour and consistency. Many were applied almost dry.

There are various accounts of San painters in South Africa using brushes made from the crushed or chewed tips of sticks, hairs from the tails of various animals, or feathers. In the Zimbabwe paintings paint was applied in various ways. In the infills of some of the largest paintings the marks of the artist's finger tips are still visible; others show evidence of the strokes of broad brushes with stiff coarse tips. But the delicacy, the uninterrupted lengths of some lines, the modulations of their thickness, the lack of any misjudgements or of dripping or spilling paint, show that many artists used brushes with very fine points that held a substantial reservoir of paint and gave them total flexibility and control over every brush stroke.

Principles

The basic feature of the art of Zimbabwe is that it is an art of outline, to such an extent that one can consider it an art based on drawing rather than painting. Colour filled the space within the outline and little more; it was not used to describe the actual appearance of the subject and people and animals could all be painted in every possible colour. White paint was sometimes used to bring out some of the distinctive differences in the colour of some animals' coats: white stomachs or undersides of some antelopes, light stripes on a kudu's back, the white circle of a waterbuck's rump and the facial markings of sable,

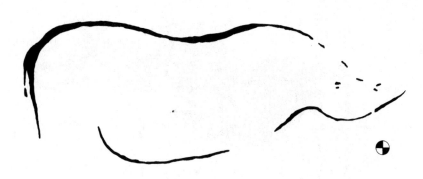

17 *The incomplete outline of a rhinoceros. Mazowe.*

but only the particularly striking markings of zebra and giraffe were illustrated with any frequency. Most paintings were in a single uniform colour: pure monochromes, profiles or silhouettes. This meant that when artists sought to indicate elements that were normally concealed within the overall body outline, these had to be transposed to the edge of the body, to break this outline. They had to be shown standing free of the body. Thus the legs of an animal lying down, although bent as in life, were not tucked in against its body but shown extending below the body, a man's penis and a woman's breasts were shown erect and projecting from the body outline and an elephant's ears were transposed to the top of its head and shown there in their entirety.

A system of multiple viewpoints was adopted so that each element of a subject was clearly visible, readily legible and easily outlined. This has been called a system of 'twisted perspective'. A person's head, face, legs and feet were shown from the side, in profile; the shoulders and body were often shown from the front, breasts or penis from the side. An animal's body and head were painted from the side,

18 *The outline of a large rhino pierced by many arrows. Goromonzi.*

19 *The outline of another rhino, partially infilled. Guruve.*

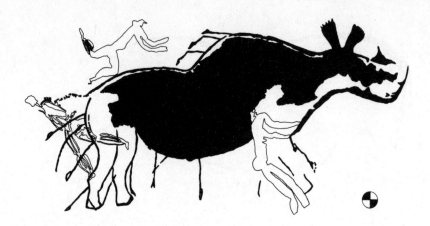

its ears and cloven hoofs, if it had them, from the front. A kudu bull's horns, spiralling out from its head, and a buffalo's horns, curving down and out from the head, were shown from the front; so were an elephant's tusks. Horns that slope or curve backwards, like those of an eland, sable or waterbuck, were shown from the side and one behind the other. A warthog's tusks were shown from above. Crocodiles were painted from above or below to capture the full swelling curves of their bellies and show all four legs, normally obscured when they are viewed from the side. In an extension of this principle, groups of people and herds of animals are shown with each individual complete and distinct, with little or no overlap between them, giving them maximum exposure and legibility at the expense of any sense of coherence, density or mass of a herd.

Any sense of the play of light or shade on the curves and muscles of a body or of the texture of a coat, of background, atmosphere or context is absent. Size, if not entirely random, was a measure of the artist's skill: in general, the better the artist, the bigger his paintings. Size was never used to give any sense of recession, distance or perspective. It was sometimes used to emphasise the importance of

20 *A grubbing warthog. Three different viewpoints have been used for body, hooves and tusks. Murewa.*

particular human figures, to enable the most intricate designs to be fully realised or to dramatise the power of the largest animals.

A few South African paintings show animals from the front or back with their bodies foreshortened, thus anticipating, in a simple way, the system of geometric perspective from a single viewpoint that was employed in Western art for almost 500 years from the Renaissance until the introduction of Cubism, and the system with which we are most familiar. Foreshortening was not developed or used anywhere in Zimbabwe.

Without the geometry, receding planes and fixed point perspective of Western art, the artists were able to spread their images across their single flat picture plane. Compositions have no boundaries, no single focus of attention, no points of balance. This meant that new images could be readily added to those that already existed, to establish new relationships between them and thus to reinterpret or elucidate their significance.

The proportions of a great many subjects were distorted, particularly by elongation of their bodies. This is so widespread and becomes so familiar that when an animal or person is shown with realistic proportions, it seems unnaturally short or compact. There is, of course, no way that we can know how the artists' societies viewed their paintings, whether they perceived them as realistic or stylised. Arguably the paintings can be considered not as illustrations but as a system in which every subject was reduced to its essential components and these were so laid out that each was fully recognisable. Subjects were reduced to their essences; the paintings are intellectual distillations of concepts of reality.

But this was not all they were. Steeped in a knowledge of animals and their behaviour, the artists realised their close observation of their subjects in their paintings. These evidence great insight and understanding of every detail of an animal, the ways it stood and moved, its physical condition and probably the ways this reflected particular seasons of the year; its mood, its sexual receptiveness, the

21 *A line of incomplete kudu, all only partially infilled. The leading cow lacks a hind leg, an indication of the process used to construct images in this art. Bindura.*

22 *A crocodile seen from below to emphasise its belly. It is decorated with white lines like those painted on people to represent strings of beads. Murewa.*

23 *Kudu painted by two different artists. The bodies of the cows are elongated, their necks thickened and dewlap hair exaggerated. In contrast it is the bull's neck that is elongated. Marondera.*

24 *An elongated man holding a fly whisk. Northern Makonde.*

ways it signalled its intentions, the degrees of its alertness, fear, aggressiveness or strength. These were reproduced with great simplicity but also accuracy and vividness. The paintings convey very strongly this sense of life and movement. Outlines were much more than modes of description. They are tense with a distilled, living energy. Almost every image is fresh and creative, individual and beautiful.

Many have been so charmed by these aspects of the art, by the apparent overwhelming naturalism of it and by its aesthetic appeal, that they have failed to recognise that, like the art of every other tradition, it was carefully governed by strict rules, that derive from the tradition, which determined the style and gave its images significance in the societies for which they were created.

Styles

If the term style is used in a broad sense, as the expression of an ideology or an epoch, then the style of the rock paintings of Zimbabwe is a single unchanging whole. If the term is used in the restricted sense of an aggregate of ready-made formal devices, there can be little doubt that the art witnessed many changes in style, both regional and temporal. Many authorities on the rock art of southern Africa have tried to discern different styles of painting and to place these in chronological sequences. Styles have been described using models established for the prehistoric caves of Europe (for example, in assigning animals in 'strict silhouette', showing only the two legs closest to the viewer, to a very early style). Some have defined styles by colour or techniques (for example, paintings in solid colour are assigned to a different style to those in outline), others describe them in terms of general impressions (such as 'classical', 'geometric', 'natu-

25 *A hunter and gatherer, by different artists yet both extremely elongated. She has bags slung from her shoulders and tassels on her knees. Murewa.*

26 *Two hunters in very different 'styles'. The small figure on the right imitates the style of its larger neighbour. Northern Makonde.*

ralistic' or 'impressionistic'). All these so-called styles are ill-defined, generalised, based on very small samples and highly subjective, to an extent that they cannot either be identified with any certainty or placed in any consistent sequences by anyone but their inventors. Later authorities have disregarded questions of style, seeing them as a waste of time and effort and a 'red herring'.

An attempt has been made to distinguish regional variations not through style but by analysing differences in the emphases given to different subjects in different areas. But this has not yet proved fruitful. It has depended on unreliable observations with too many misidentifications and misinterpretations of the subjects, samples that were too small and categories – like animal species – that were too broad.

In tackling questions of stylistic variation, there are problems defining what constitutes a style, what interrelated sets of definable formal differences are significant. One must recognise that formal differences may reflect various factors: individual artists' idiosyncracies, abilities and skills; regional schools of interacting artists limited to small areas and short periods; distinction in the functions and significance of different categories of paintings, the possibility that at any one time and place, artists used different techniques and took varying degrees of care when they painted different subjects or themes. It is comparatively easy to identify the works of individual artists and, to a lesser extent, small local schools of artists. It is readily noticeable, for instance, that different artists handled the shapes, proportions and articulations of heads and limbs very differently. Such dissimilarities cannot yet be said to constitute the characteristics of distinct styles. I am at present unable to distinguish different styles

27 *Small peripheral sketches by inexpert artists, as a comparison with fig. 5 shows. Despite their crudeness, the painters of the sables are aware of the principles of the art that insist that all parts of the body are shown with only minimal overlaps. Mazowe.*

of painting in the art. Thus although there are formal variations in the art, their significance is uncertain and their parameters cannot be satisfactorily defined.

One of the many unquestioned assertions that has been attached to the art is that only the most skilled artists, the 'masters', were permitted to paint on rock and only their works have been preserved. It is assumed that lesser artists and those not yet fully competent painted and practised on impermanent materials such as bark or hide. This idea lives on today in suggestions that only trancers painted on rock.

In fact a whole range of skills and talents is apparent in the surviving paintings. It is possible to distinguish the work of unskilled painters in the many small sketches of static figures done with uncertain, hesitant brush strokes, forming crude wavering lines with random changes in thickness and which bear no relationship to form. They seem to be placed consistently round the edges of painted panels. Elements of many of these figures are disproportionately, indeed enormously, exaggerated, perhaps especially the genital organs. Despite their lacks, the painters of these sketches had nevertheless absorbed the principles of the art. They understood and mastered the use of multiple viewpoints. Working within a developed visual tradition, they were attempting to reproduce other paintings, not nature in the raw. These isolated little images show few of the skills, the complete control of brush, medium and line, the modulations, detail and conviction of the better paintings and lack the ability to capture and suggest movement, or the repetition of images to form whole compositions, that mark more accomplished paintings. The activities these little sketches illustrate are more varied – and earthier; only in such paintings are there scenes of, for instance, animated conversations, eating, copulation or sodomy.

The pre-eminent early authorities, Frobenius and Breuil, both recognised something of the differences in skills shown in the paintings. Both however interpreted this as distinguishing the work of primitive 'Bushmen' from that of artists of a very different race and culture who had migrated to the region from some high civilisation far to the north. Reality may be much more mundane. It may well be that these small peripheral paintings are the work of children, learning about and intrigued by many different aspects of life and art. The great range of skills apparent in the paintings tallies with San practices today. In San societies anyone may attempt anything; nothing is esoteric. Children learn skills from imitating through play and participating as far as they are able in adult activities and are given every encouragement to do so.

These sketches at least serve to widen the range of the art, for while the total subject matter was extensive, the most important and skilled

28 *A sketch of a man with a disproportionately enlarged emblem on his penis. Northern Makonde.*

29 *A variation on the sketch above. Northern Makonde.*

30 *A poorly drawn little sketch apparently of men engaged in egregious sexual practices. Harare.*

paintings exhibit a narrower and more restricted range of concerns. But all this is still far from defining significant regional or temporal variations. That can only come later when the concerns of the paintings are more clearly understood, and may prove difficult. The art is so homogeneous and significant changes so difficult to discern, that it may well prove that the paintings now preserved were executed over a comparatively short span of time within the very wide parameters that now delimit the dates of the paintings.

1

APPROACHES TO THE ART

Experts from Europe

Most students of the rock art of Zimbabwe have been authorities from abroad. Locals have taken these as their mentors, an inevitability an in a country which has never had the institutions to stimulate new forms of enquiry or provide the informed exchanges of ideas from which research could develop. The first attempts to understand the paintings looked to the earliest theories that had been developed in Europe to explain the prehistoric cave paintings of France and Spain. These proposed that these paintings were believed to have magical powers which enabled the artists to influence the animals they painted, either to make them more fertile and increase the herds or to give hunters power over them so that they might find and kill them more easily. Such ideas have had a long life but no one has been able to show that there are any specific features of the imagery to support them or any indications of the presence of such beliefs in any societies in Africa.

In 1927, Miles Burkitt of Cambridge University, one of the first and best known lecturers in prehistoric archaeology in Britain, travelled through southern Africa to identify the problems, promote research and help to bring order to the infant discipline of archaeology in the region. For him, the rock paintings had no more intellectual or cultural significance than wallpaper, with which he compared them. They changed over the centuries in response to no more than whim or fashion.[7] Their only interest was the problems raised by their chronology and associations with the stone tools found in the soils beneath them, problems which would be resolved by the orderly methods of archaeology, establishing a classification and typology of styles and a chronological sequence. Current priorities in the research reveal the limitations of this view which, however, dominated the approaches to the art of Zimbabwe for a great many years to the extent that no one seemed able to recognise that there was a great deal more to the art than a set of archaeological problems. Indeed, the concerns of traditional archaeology scarcely impinged at all on the understanding of the nature and significance of the art.

In 1928, Leo Frobenius, already long established as Germany's best known explorer, collector, cultural historian and ethnographer of Africa, brought a team of artists and archaeologists to the region, to pursue his research into his long-held theories that all African 'high culture' was a residue of ancient civilisations developed beyond her shores.

Frobenius focused on one section of the paintings of Zimbabwe and named it the 'Wedge Style'. The number of types of images in the style was really very small, forming a 'self-contained unity'. The 'strong, relentless purity' of style showed in an 'astonishingly clearly controlled, self-contained and self-assured certainty of form'. It had a 'dourness … severity … discipline and seriousness'. He distinguished this style of painting in many fundamental ways from the main body of 'Bushman paintings'. Human figures in this Wedge Style show the body including the shoulders from the front and the limbs and head in profile, producing the characteristic wedge-shaped torso. Some heads had a pronounced muzzle which he interpreted as a mask; others were separated from the body and others reduced to 'small buttons'. The positions of the limbs were often 'affected and mannered'. Some figures assumed a characteristic posture, leaning slightly back or forward with their legs close together, so that they appeared to be 'floating' and ghost-like. Others were limbless or originally had limbs painted in evanescent white pigment. The most important of the human figures were those that were recumbent and carefully composed with minor figures around them. Frobenius interpreted these as representing dead kings with their mourners and named them 'pietas'. Paintings of animals lacked the 'verisimilitude', 'pure literal realism' and 'faithfulness to nature' that are found in paintings in South Africa and are popularly taken to be a feature of San art. They were derived or copied from other paintings rather than from life. Some figures were entirely artificial creations; these included figures with pointed muzzles, long pointed ears and 'onion-shaped' bodies from which the arms and legs 'stuck out', which he named 'mythical hares'. Lines, apparently representing water or urine, emerged from between their legs and they were sometimes

31 *The large figures, of striking economy and elegance, are in Frobenius' 'Wedge Style'. Women as gatherers are signified simply by their breasts and digging sticks. Marondera.*

32 *A distended figure with legs and arms apart, of the sort that Frobenius designated 'mythical hares'. Guruve.*

surrounded by dots. Other creatures had the bodies of snakes but their heads also had large ears and their backs were cusped, like 'hills', and people walked along these or hung suspended from the snakes' heads.[8]

A 'truly essential and fundamental feature' of the style was the painting of landscapes. Trees were often surrounded by fields of dots which Frobenius took to represent pools, lakes, rivers and rain. Most important of all were geometric designs based on ovals, 'shapes of cigars with a good length of ash [at one end]', which Frobenius took to represent the granite boulders of the Zimbabwe landscape. But, he emphasised, these designs were not copies of nature but 'natural objects with symbolic meaning', a symbol 'not only outwardly and formally but above all as a symptom of [the style's] psyche, its essential being'. This was most true of the ovals but applied to all the images in this style. The landscapes were 'not copies of nature but natural objects with a symbolic meaning'. Images of animals had 'not come from nature but rather from imaginative experience'; the hares, snakes and ghost figures belonged to a mythical world. The recumbent figures represented the central theme of the art, 'an expression of [man's] fate or destiny'. All the key images were essentially anchored in an inner vision, derived from the imagination, and bore no relation to daily life. All expressed the mystical in symbol.

Frobenius claimed to recognise a graphic technique specific to the Wedge Style. He asserted that paintings in this style were begun without outlines, in sets of fine stripes and that the artists, unlike those of later periods, always worked from left to right. Outlines were added last, almost all being in a single colour, red, and many subject to rich over-painting and over-working in white. Apparently different shades and hues of red were the result of subsequent action by the

33 *A 'geometric design' of the type that Frobenius saw as representing landscapes. Mazowe.*

1 *The long slope up to one of the larger caves in Zimbabwe. Paintings in it are illustrated in plates* xxv *and* xxxvi.
In the middle distance, the hills are strewn with granite boulders. On the horizon are more great granite 'whale backs'.
Matobo.

II *(above) The dark horizontal slit of a large cave breaks the slopes of a granite 'whale back'. Paintings in this cave are illustrated in plates XI, XXVI and XXVII. Mutoko.*

III *(right) Split and weathered granite boulders, the 'balancing rocks' so characteristic of the Zimbabwean countryside. Their forms were once considered the origin of the 'oval designs' in the paintings. Matobo.*

IV (above) The smooth 'semi-dome' of a large painted cave. Some of the paintings in it are illustrated in plate XIII. Matobo.

V (left) Tracing paintings of a scene of people encamped. Mutoko.

VI (left) A variety of
animals painted at
different times by different
artists. This site is typical of
many hundreds in
Zimbabwe. The kudu bull
on the right is reproduced as
fig. 2. Marondera.

VII (below) A painted
boulder wedged beneath and
protected by a much larger
one. The paintings are few,
weathered and abraded but
of great interest. They are
reproduced as fig. 87.
Harare.

VIII *The small dark antelope are painted with greater skill and more exact observation than the unfinished red painting of a tsessebe. One is an extremely rare example of a painting that has subsequently been altered; here the position of the head has been changed. Makonde.*

IX (above) Part of a long frieze, another part of which is illustrated on the endpapers: kudu bulls superimposed on a long speckled and multi-coloured snake-like line. The outlines of the legs of a large elephant intrude. Bindura.

X (opposite above) The two felines painted here are characteristically so small and imprecise that the species is indeterminate. A recumbent human figure, another in white and a cross-hatched antelope are distinguishable around them. Mutoko.

XI (opposite below) Paintings damaged by exfoliation. The dark outline, embellished with white dots, of an ochre elephant; an antelope painted upside down, though its body is still tense with life; and undulating lines with semi-human figures crawling along them; all demand interpretation. Mutoko.

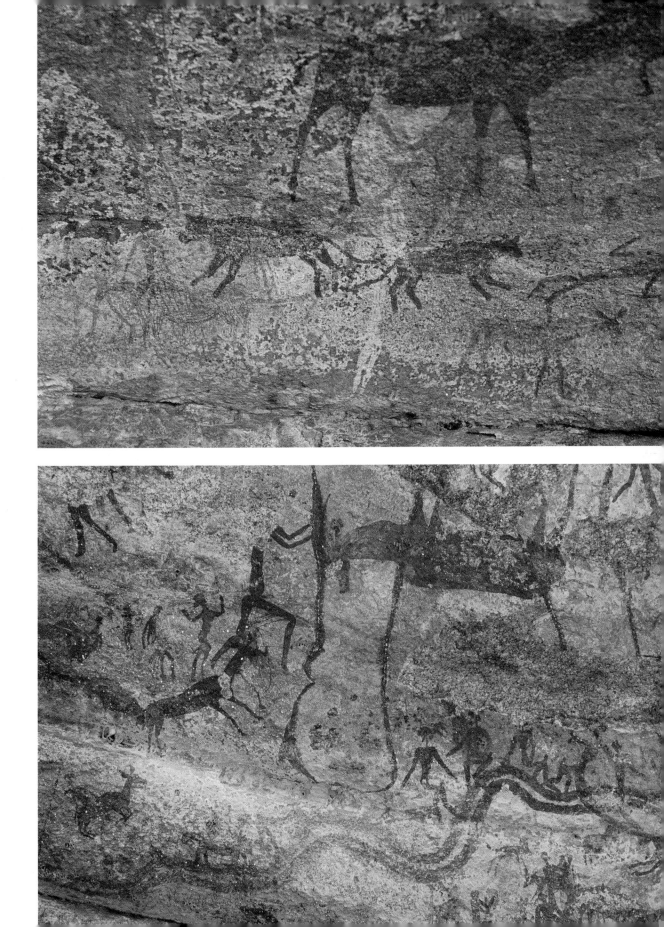

XII (above) Part of a particularly long frieze of kudu cows moving at a fast walk. Their elongated bodies are beautifully observed and carefully outlined in white. Above, bands of hunters are moving towards each other equally fast. The coloured line painted at the top also extends across the whole cave and has its origin in a fault in the rock. Ndanga.

XIII (below) This frieze of large, dark figures typifies some of the major concerns of the artists. Along the top, trancers hold their heads, lie supine or heal a patient by massaging his or her back. In the centre women in their shelters care for their children and grind food. Along the bottom, men prepare their equipment and set out for the hunt. Below is a series of delicate, detailed and colourful images of creatures with a snake's body and a kudu's head. Matobo.

elements. Yellow pigment was only introduced as the style deteriorated.

Frobenius had wider and more prolonged first-hand field experience of the paintings of Zimbabwe and South Africa than anyone else before or since. Others now know the paintings of their particular areas of study much better than he did but no one has yet been in a good position to compare the paintings of the various regions of southern Africa. The distinctions he makes between them carry weight. He was the first and is still almost the only authority to base his work on detailed comparative analytical studies of the paintings of southern Africa as a whole. He based his studies on a very large and very good collection of accurate copies; eschewing broad and unsubstantiated generalisations about the art, he instead supported his conclusions with a range of specific examples taken from the paintings themselves. The features of the paintings of Zimbabwe that he isolated and defined are indeed the most significant in the art – the oval designs, the fields of flecks, their association with trees, the

34 *Paintings of the sort that Frobenius accepted as painted by 'Bushmen' and depicting their activities. Two men enter an antbear burrow while their companions wait with sticks above; two richly apparelled women dance. Other figures fall and lie back with lines streaming from their heads. Mazowe.*

distended and recumbent figures, the floating figures and those with pointed muzzles and large ears. His insights into the essential nature of the art, its basis in the expression of concepts derived from belief and from the mind, and in a prescribed vocabulary of visual forms, remain valid and must form the basis for understanding.

But whereas Frobenius saw his Wedge Style as sharply different from the rest of the paintings in Zimbabwe, it was not the work of a distinct people nor of a different period. This was a hypothesis he never tested by examining the positions of paintings in this style in the sequence of superpositioning and thus demonstrating conclusively that they were always earlier than those in other styles. It is likely that paintings in this 'style' were the work of the most skilled artists, masters both of their craft and its techniques and also of the system of signification that was the basis of the art. Because of their mastery in these fields, they were able to focus on the most difficult, central, metaphysical themes of both belief and its visual representation. Their art is nevertheless embedded in a much wider corpus of paintings which explore every aspect of life in the artists' societies, both the trivial and the significant. Having created his artificial distinctions of attribution, style, period, culture and people within the art, Frobenius could not understand the significance in San terms of the imagery of his Wedge Style, although he recognised that San painting in South Africa was based fundamentally in 'shamanism'.

Anthropologists and historians have been harshly critical of Frobenius' relationships with the people he was studying, of his methods of fieldwork, and of the ways he collected information, folklore and traditions. His work has been ignored, at least in southern Africa and the English-speaking world, for over sixty years, partly because no one working in the field read German, but also because Frobenius set his Wedge Style in a context that was unacceptable to anyone with knowledge of southern African prehistory. He used it as evidence to support theories about the origins of Great Zimbabwe in cultural elements from distant places in a distant past. Frobenius asserted that the style had developed originally as fresco painting on the plastered walls of graves and royal enclosures such as Great Zimbabwe and had only later spread and been preserved on the rock surfaces. It was a manifestation of a 'high culture' that could be traced from current Shona burial practices and mythology, through to the local Mutapa state of the sixteenth century AD, and back to a mythic Muetsi empire, whose beliefs were rooted in the movements of the moon and Venus, which determined the ritual sacrifice of the empire's kings, and thence to 'Erythraa' and remote origins in the ancient civilisations of western Asia. The paintings were used to give substance to theories about the immense antiquity

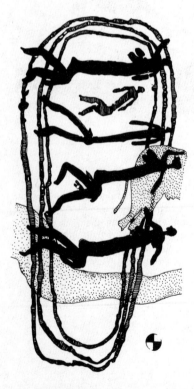

35 *Recumbent figures superimposed on three lines outlining an oval shape: the sort of image that Frobenius interpreted as concerned with royal burials. Murewa.*

and exotic origins of Great Zimbabwe and hence, indirectly, to emphasise the supposed decadence and backwardness of the present inhabitants of the country. These arguments submerged Frobenius' real contributions towards defining and understanding the basis of the art. In this sphere he showed extraordinary insight. He understood the ways that visual art expresses ideas. He respected the artists and their beliefs, even if he did not know who or what they were. He was a sensitive observer and a rigorous and methodical analyst who had an almost unerring eye for the significant in the art of Zimbabwe.

After his expedition, one of Frobenius' artists returned to marry and make her life in Zimbabwe. For the next forty years, Elizabeth Mannsfeld-Goodall traced paintings, building up a monumental body of work now kept in the Queen Victoria Memorial Museum in Harare. Her copies will probably never be matched for their skill, care and accuracy. They succeed more than any others in giving a sense of the character and quality of the originals though they translate these into watercolour painting on paper. Because she was completely loyal to her 'master', Frobenius, in a country where he was belittled or ignored, because she felt alienated by the arguments and entrenched positions that have always characterised southern African prehistoric studies and because she was never fully at home in English, she wrote very little about the paintings. Her few contributions were a celebration, and not an analysis, of the art.[9]

36 *Paintings adjacent to fig. 35. Goodall isolated the animal skin and the three figures below it as a 'burial scene', presumably on an analogy with the Shona custom of wrapping the corpses of some of their dead in cow hides: a conflation of two very different historical periods like that accepted by Frobenius.*

37 *A panel that includes a pair of gatherers, a line of hunters by different hands and many hunters aiming at creatures with only partial resemblances to animals of any known species. Mutoko.*

38 *Figures hold long, rigid and light objects to their faces, possibly a form of musical pipe: a recurrent image whose associations with any other imagery, and therefore its interpretations, remain uncertain. Guruve.*

Henri Breuil was one of the greatest of the pioneers in discovering, recording and studying the cave paintings of Europe. His dominance in this field was unquestioned for decades. Long and solitary eminence made him increasingly dismissive of all criticism. He visited the paintings of southern Africa at the same time as Frobenius and Burkitt, one of his first pupils and colleagues. He returned as an old man, to study some of them more thoroughly in the 1950s. Much influenced by Frobenius though he never acknowledged it, like him he was dismissive of 'Bushman paintings' and was obsessed instead with establishing that some paintings were the work of foreign immigrants – Egyptians, Minoans and 'Nilotes' of great antiquity. Their art, he speculated, might prove to be a survival of the original art of historic Egypt and Crete and hence evidence of the beginnings of the artistic tradition of the whole of Europe, the basis of much of the art of our world today. He focused particularly on figures painted in white because he believed these must represent the work of the white-skinned immigrant artists and produced a series of lavish books to try to prove his controversial thesis.[10] They were filled with unconvincing sketches of paintings that have little resemblance to the originals: fantastic figures clad in helmets, armour, cloaks and Persian slippers. Local prehistorians were saddened and silenced and were unwilling to argue with someone whose previous contributions to rock art studies they and the world so admired.

South African Authorities

A generation after the studies of rock art by Burkitt, Frobenius and Breuil, books based on an extensive use of colour photography began to appear in South Africa. A. R. Willcox led the way and remains the most persuasive proponent of the new genre. It extolled the beauty, variety and skill of the paintings, seen as the romantic residue of a vanished people and their paradise of a joyful, leisured coexistence with nature. The paintings were remembrances of the emotions and excitements of past pleasures. They were a product of the pride of artists in their skills and craftsmanship, their delight in the praise of their audiences. Their art was so simple that it was immediately comprehensible to anyone of any culture and any age. These paintings were art in its pristine purity, art executed solely for personal pleasure, art for its own sake.

These were not new ideas; in fact they were derived from a review in 1910 by a former leading British art critic, Roger Fry, of one of the first books to reproduce some of the paintings.[11] While some of these persistent ideas may be true, they do not address the way the art was structured or its significance within the culture that produced it.

In Zimbabwe, the strong influence of Willcox is apparent in the work of C. K. Cooke, Secretary and Director of the Historical Monuments Commission of Rhodesia between 1951 and 1972.[12] Initially, influenced by Burkitt, he attempted to identify and define more precisely changing styles of paintings. Later he followed Breuil, but with somewhat greater circumspection. He took a painting of sheep and their herders in north-east Zimbabwe, related it to Breuil's white paintings in the south and outside Zimbabwe, and deduced a route of pastoralist migration through southern Africa. An enthusiastic adherent to Fry's and Willcox's beliefs that the art was an immediate and direct illustration of things seen in the artists' daily lives, he treated the paintings as historical records of such things as incursions of armed warriors of different African groups, iron smelting processes or advents of plague.

Fundamentally, the work in this genre is a denial that the paintings constitute an art form in any real sense, that they have any intellectual, cultural or spiritual content. This superficial and subjective interpretation of the paintings reduces them to the level of personal anecdote and alienates them from any historical, ideological or social context. It is comparable to the interpretations one could expect of a visitor from outer space confronted with the Christian art of Europe. At best he could only describe paintings of the Nativity, life of Christ and the Crucifixion in terms of archaic clothes, fashions, domestic arrangements, maternity care and maintenance of law and order. He could know nothing of the key beliefs and concepts of Christianity, of the doctrines of the Incarnation or Redemption. He would see Christ without divinity, man without a soul.

In the 1960s and 1970s archaeologists tried to bring some objectivity and order to the field by making systematic surveys of all the paintings in defined areas and analysing every image in terms of a wide range of basic features – size, colour, orientation, subject, activity and forms – and then assessing the results statistically. This still

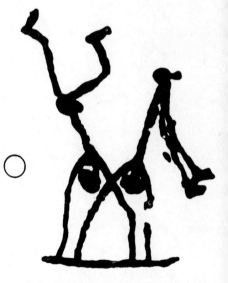

39 *Only the smallest, most inexpert and peripheral sketches in the Zimbabwe art are readily – but not necessarily correctly – interpretable as illustrations of personal anecdotes. This is the case with these apparent acrobats. Guruve.*

40 *The only painting of a line fringed with white dots known in Zimbabwe. Early in his work, Lewis-Williams interpreted similar images in South Africa, from their contexts, as 'symbolising manifestations of supernatural potency'. Northern Makonde.*

failed to give any idea of the content of the art. It could not: the categories were external creations imposed on the material, not derived from it.

Scholars of the late twentieth century, concerned with the paintings in different parts of the Drakensberg in South Africa, achieved the first real breakthrough in understanding the art.[13] These paintings are estimated to be no more than 300 years old at most and some are evidently much more recent for they depict the arrival of Boer settlers and British soldiers in the area in the mid-nineteenth century.

In twenty-five years of work, David Lewis-Williams made a series of advances that must profoundly alter everyone's perceptions of the art. In contrast to his predecessors, Lewis-Williams tried to investigate the art using the methods and logic that he believed must underlie all reputable research in whatever field. He insisted that all hypotheses about the art should be explicitly formulated, precise and verifiable against clearly stated evidence; that they should be in conformity with all that was already known about the San; that they should be coherent, economic and simplifying, creative yet sufficiently dynamic in the sense of being capable of generating further hypotheses of the same sort.[14]

His first papers showed that the paintings followed definite rules about which subjects could be painted over which. There was a 'structure' and 'syntax' to the art that had no relationship to the visible world.[15] He then examined and interpreted the few recorded discussions about particular paintings by San near-neighbours and contemporaries of the Drakensberg artists and showed how they understood the paintings as visual illustrations of San metaphors for their experiences of trancing. Re-examination of the much more extensive nineteenth-century records of the beliefs and folklore of the Xam San of the northern Cape and subsequently of the more recent and much more detailed and systematic anthropological studies of the few remaining hunters and foragers among the Kung San of north-west Botswana showed that they shared very similar beliefs, practices and metaphors. The paintings could now be placed in a precise cultural context. A large corpus of material – visual, historical, oral, anthropological and ritual – could now be used to help interpret them.[16]

Lewis-Williams' interpretations of small paintings found in South Africa on slabs of stone that had been incorporated in dated archaeological deposits some two or three millennia old and his interpretations of copies of some paintings in Tanzania suggested to him that their artists shared the same concerns, metaphors and imagery as those who worked in the Drakensberg. It was thus possible to speak of a 'pan-San cognitive system' that had existed over a very wide

41 *Among these figures are apparent swaying, falling and recumbent figures, an incomplete figure and an attenuated figure holding his chest, all of which Lewis-Williams would interpret as illustrating aspects of trancing. There is also a family group and lines of hunters and gatherers which have no obvious reference to trancing. All are superimposed on the outline of a very large rhinoceros. Goromonzi.*

geographical area and a long period of time.[17] This seemed to find striking confirmation when copies of Drakensberg paintings were shown to some Kung San hunters. Though the Kung are not themselves painters, they immediately understood these paintings in the ways that Lewis-Williams had deduced.[18]

Apparently, all San believed that prolonged communal dances could induce trancing, which enabled trancers – or shamans as Lewis-Williams now prefers to call them – to generate, harness and release their innate spiritual energy or potency. Lewis-Williams is increasingly emphatic that paintings in southern Africa are the work of shamans and illustrate their experiences in trance. For Lewis-Williams all paintings have at least a coded reference to some aspect of trance or potency. The key to the code lies in San descriptions of trance. Using this key will eventually enable the entire art to be decoded.[19]

With Thomas Dowson, he advanced further to assert that many simple painted forms – like clusters of lines, curves, dots and zig-zags – illustrate what they call 'entoptics': neuropsychological phenomena brought on by trancing and experienced not through the eye or mind but through direct stimulation of the nervous system. Conflations of this imagery with more detailed and recognisable animal or human figures illustrate visions experienced in deeper levels of trance. Such hallucinations are common to all people whatever their cultural background. Thus wherever paintings illustrating them occur, as in the caves of Europe, they can be interpreted in the same way. Shamanism can be taken to have been a widespread phenomenon and used to explain many prehistoric paintings throughout the world and even the origin of art itself.[20]

Most recently, Lewis-Williams has accepted the word of a very elderly associate of long dead San artists that the very paints they used were potent, that paintings were more than images of potency: they were potent in themselves.[21] More, the rock surfaces on which the images were painted were only a 'veil' separating the shaman artists from the spirit world, one rendered transparent by trance so that the paintings were a direct revelation of a spirit world behind the rock surface. In Lewis-Williams' view this concept of the art was supported by paintings that seemed to have been deliberately placed so that they seem to emerge from and disappear into minor irregularities in the rock surface.[22]

Zimbabwe

It would be a mistake to transpose interpretations developed from the Drakensberg paintings simply and directly to Zimbabwe. The former are at most a few centuries old while the age of the latter must be measured in millennia. The art of Zimbabwe seems a great deal more varied in subject and treatment. It includes much imagery entirely unrepresented further south. Compositions in Zimbabwe are more complex in their relationships, associations and layering. But however considerable the differences, indubitably both belong to the same tradition. Both can be assumed to reflect the same San 'cognitive system', the same ways of seeing, of interpreting what is seen, of concepts and basic beliefs and practices.

The Drakensberg San paintings benefit from near-contemporary recorded evidence; this is not the case in Zimbabwe where no established San societies have lived near the paintings for many centuries. Except through their paintings and the archaeological debris of their food and tools, nothing is known of them, still less of their beliefs. The San of Zimbabwe formed a very distinct entity, living in a different environment from those to the south or west, responding to the local vegetation and animal life with different methods of hunting and probably having different methods of social organisation. Their perceptions and beliefs, moulded by such factors, would also have changed over the centuries though we may as yet be unable to distinguish this in their art.

Our work must be informed by what we can tease out of the essence of the perceptions and beliefs common to all known San groups. At the same time, it would be a grave mistake to set the paintings of Zimbabwe in an unchanging San present, an artificial

42 *Two hunters superimposed on a small distended figure, squatting above three lines that constitute part of her imagery. Mutoko.*

invention of anthropologists who only know small groups of living San hunters. It is even more mistaken to play what have been called 'games of ethnographic snap', to isolate individual images which we think we understand and match them to particular San practices or beliefs known only from nineteenth- or twentieth-century ethnographies. We must rather seek out, disentangle and isolate those images that hint at differences from the San that anthropologists know.

For this we can rely only on evidence from the paintings themselves. This demands first a very close study of them. In my own experience this can only be achieved through exact tracing of every detail of a large number of paintings, an arduous, uncomfortable and prolonged process but one that also forces one into long and intimate contact with each painting, during which one also has time to think about each image and, largely subconsciously perhaps, place it in a context. In practice these processes are not distinct or successive but closely integrated. At the same time comparisons between paintings facilitate both the isolation of different genres, themes, sets of images and motifs and recognition of their common features, their variations and range of variations. One begins to recognise a range of details – signs, motifs, attributes or emblems – that seem to have served to signify or define particular qualities. Regular patterns of association between emblems and images helps one to suggest what these qualities may have been. One also begins to identify the canon of the art, what was regularly represented and, just as important, what was seldom, if ever, painted. As the process continues, one is also able to begin to construct or reconstruct the ways that objects could be described, represented or reproduced – the principles that constitute style. In all of this, it is the images that are primary, their principles, canon, themes, associations and elements. It is essential to have some grasp of all of this – of what constitutes the art – before an attempt is made to integrate it with the fundamentals of the San mind.

43 *Two armed men. The shapes added to their heads, shoulders, buttocks and penises and the forms of their arrowheads can all be interpreted as emblems of invisible or supernatural qualities. Guruve.*

This is a different process from the statistical analyses of archaeologists. Recognition and definition of significant attributes derives from the close comparative study of selected images or panels of paintings; it is not imposed by the preconceptions of the archaeologist's mind. Statistical analyses may one 0day be used to test and refine interpretations suggested here but they cannot in themselves provide them. This is also a different process, with different prior-

44 *The large outline of a buffalo on which are superimposed a group of 'pipers'. Their pipes, zig-zag arms and most unusual if not unique tasselled genital organs all require interpretation. They overlie a little group of four aproned women, more easily recognizable as dancers. Mazowe.*

ities, from those used elsewhere in the study of other periods where it is easy to match image with belief, one for one.

One must from the first approach the art with respect, aware that however apparently simple a culture's technology or worldly goods, the way it thought about, classified and categorised and made sense of its world may be complex. Once preconceptions are discarded, one soon recognises that San art is probably as rich as any in allusions and evocations, metaphor and symbol. It is rich conceptually too, having developed sophisticated modes of visually representing abstract ideas and concepts. If this is the case, it cannot be simplified by reduction to a form of language, still less a code: the visual and oral are very different modes of communication, and one cannot be equated with or transposed to the other. One can describe and analyse visual representations in words but it is simplistic to claim to define fully a painting's meaning in words. One cannot read art; one can only explore aspects of significance.

However limited its canon, the art of Zimbabwe still seems to celebrate or explore a greater range of concerns than the art of the Drakensberg. It uses a greater variety of methods – particularly metaphors and symbols of invisible worlds and powers. Metaphor and symbol have in theory been recognised as important in the art of South Africa but in practice interpretations describe a much more directly illustrative content in the south than in the north. At the same time, the art of the south illustrates less.

It will become clear that I have recognised in Zimbabwe no illustrations of various forms or degrees of entoptic hallucinations and little that directly illustrates the spirit world. Dancing, trancers and healers had as important a place in the Zimbabwean art as they did in the life of all San groups but they were by no means the sole concerns of the artists: many other aspects of life were explored. Symbols of potency are perhaps the most striking, complex and important images among the paintings and can be said to pervade the art in various forms as they pervade San life. These differences – primarily differences of emphasis – do not indicate that current interpretations of paintings outside Zimbabwe are necessarily wrong. Rather they demonstrate that there were variations in artistic concerns and expression which are only to be expected in paintings so very different in place and time.

The paintings of Zimbabwe cannot be interpreted within a single sweeping overall explanation nor do they all illustrate different aspects of shamanism. They address a broader range of concerns and explore almost every aspect of society and its ideology, focusing on the nature and actions of every form of potency rather than on the experiences of trance. They mobilise a greater range of visual tools

45 *A zebra juxtaposed with a recumbent figure. A conceptual relationship between these two seemingly incongruous images should be sought. Marondera.*

than those in South Africa, shifting the emphasis from illustration towards careful intellectual constructs of symbols operating on deeper levels. Where South African paintings are said to illustrate the spirit world, in Zimbabwe, while there may well be paintings representing gods and spirits, creation and generation, these are visual constructs of invisible objects. Where many simple motifs in South Africa are presented as illustrations of entoptics, similar motifs in Zimbabwe seem better explained as rational constructs and visual expressions of ideas and beliefs, not of sensations. Where paintings in South Africa are interpreted as simple encodings, those in Zimbabwe have richer symbolic resonances and are not susceptible to such simple readings. It would be difficult to sustain that the paintings in Zimbabwe were all the work of shamans; they exhibit much too broad a range of skills and competence.

How far do these differences of interpretation represent real differences in the imagery? How far do they reflect differences in the 'mind-sets' of the researchers who developed them? It is almost certainly a bit of both. But at present it is impossible to know. Neither myself nor David Lewis-Williams has seen work in any region but his own and for information from outside we have to rely on published material. Indeed no serious student of the art since Frobenius has made a serious comparative study of the painting of southern Africa as a whole.

As can already be seen, there are considerable methodological differences between Lewis-Williams and me, in large part forced by the differing nature of the material with which we work. Both believe in the coherence of the art or the artistic system as a whole. We differ in that I do not share his belief in a single, overarching, determining principle or explanation for the art. In crude terms, I give the image primacy and Lewis-Williams the anthropology of the San. I locate the study of the art within the humanities, as an aspect of art history or iconography, using methods similar to those of many other art historians. Lewis-Williams sees the study of these paintings as a science, as an aspect of what he calls and professes 'cognitive archaeology', placing great stress on theory building and testing in ways used by all scientists. He denies any role for the pragmatic or empirical. I see the process of interpretation as more closely comparable with that practised by a medical doctor who starts from a foundation of sound scientific knowledge of human physiology, psychology and pathology, just as any student of the paintings must start with an understanding of San anthropology. As a doctor examines an individual patient's general pattern of health and seeks anomalies, 'symptoms', within this, a student of the art should scan and understand the general pattern of the imagery, seek patterns within this, recognise regularities and anomalies. On these both base their 'diagnoses', interpretation and recognition of significance. In both cases, the process is one that is very largely pragmatic, empirical and intuitive. It must therefore also be based on wide experience. Laboratory tests on a patient, like statistical analyses of the paintings, may be employed subsequently to confirm diagnosis, but diagnosis comes first, the focusing of the mind on one particular area of concern. It seems as likely that there is a single overarching explanation for the paintings as that there is a single cause of illness. Advances in understanding something of the paintings, as in understanding a patient's problems, are more likely to result from a progressive series of small steps, developing and testing many small hypotheses. When their validity seems firm, they can be used as the bases for further minor excursions and advances.

2

THE HUMAN IMAGE AS ARCHETYPE

The Hunter

The dominant image among the paintings of Zimbabwe, at least numerically, is that of the male hunter. Tall, slender and naked, he was painted singly or in parties of up to forty very similar figures. His torso is long and generally curved forward, delineated with hard, straight lines and showing his broad shoulders. His buttocks are small but well defined. His penis projects almost horizontally from his body; his scrotum is very seldom shown. His legs are sharply divided into thighs and muscular calves, and he has small feet with rounded heels and high insteps. Fingers and toes as well as facial features – nose, mouth or eyes – are very seldom visible. His head is often a simple circular or oval shape, on top of a long neck, but more commonly, his forehead is a large rounded boss, sharply distinguished from the face below it, which is a projecting rectangular shape rather like an animal's muzzle. This is no mask but the consequence of the way that artists conceptualised the head.

Men's heads frequently bear elaborate additions: lines hanging down over the back of the neck, lines standing upright across the crown, similar lines parted in the middle, single large triangular or cone shapes on the top of the head or a series of 'tufts' across the head with narrow stems and wide splayed ends. The penis often has a line or bar across it or a sinuous line coming out of the end of it. A similar

46 *A typical hunter. Goromonzi.*

47 *Hunters with their weapons and hunting bags beside them. Harare.*

line can instead be attached to the upper tip of the bar. These lines also end in a splayed-out, tufted shape.

The hunter carries a simple curved bow that is generally about half his height but it can sometimes be four times this long. In one hand he holds between two and six arrows, usually denoted by a single brush stroke. While most arrows thus seem to have been no more than simple wooden shafts with one end sharpened to a point, many are sharply thickened at the butt, the end carried lowest and closest to the body. This suggests they had some form of flight. In fig. 47 asymmetric loops have been added to the butts of the arrows that two of the hunters carry. In fig. 48 the butts are bulbous and hold a nicked tip to fit into the bow string. Most arrows have no indication that they had separate heads but two paintings show hunters binding arrowheads to the shafts of their arrows with some form of twine. In one of these, another hunter is shown stringing his bow. There is a distinct group of extremely large and elaborate arrowheads, formed of several lines, usually in the form of a large transverse cross or a triangle with the broad base pointing forward and the tip of the triangle attached to the shaft. Many of these have at least one long barb between the head and the shaft.

Much more rarely men are armed with short clubs with heavy heads with which they attack small animals. Others have long thin sticks and use these to probe burrows and extract small creatures that have taken refuge within them. A few men carry smoothly rounded oval objects that may represent stone missiles, though they are never depicted throwing them. The men with clubs, sticks or stones are seldom shown in hunting parties. Theirs was, as far as the paintings show, an unusual and generally solitary activity.

48 *A detail from fig. 82. The hunters' arrows have unusually elaborate butts. Makonde.*

49 *The hunter on the left binds a head to his arrow. Murewa.*

50 *The hunter second from the left strings his bow. The bindings of the arrows held by the hunter on the right are visible. Mazowe.*

Most hunters carry a small bag with a narrow neck, slung high on one shoulder by a looped handle. In it there are several more arrows, placed head down, and a fly whisk with its thick serrated end hanging out of the bag. Much less often, hunters have a long tubular quiver instead of a bag.

51 *Two men use a stick to probe an animal burrow. Mutoko.*

The Gatherer

Women were painted far less often than men. Their bodies are plumper and more rounded and often their buttocks are larger and their lower backs more deeply curved than a man's. Their elongated breasts project one above the other. They often wear tasselled aprons over their buttocks and sometimes have a second apron in front. Sometimes the complete skins of small animals hang over their backs as capes; these can be tied in the small of their backs to form large bags, the legs of the skins tied round their bodies and hanging down in front. Occasionally they were used to carry their babies. Many women also carry long sticks.

Bags and sticks denote the women's principal economic activity – digging for roots or water and gathering food. While hunters appear in large parties and vigorous movement, gatherers set out in smaller groups and do not move at more than a sedate walk. Sometimes a child may go with them.

On rare occasions, a woman is shown squatting within an enclosure, indicated by a long curved line and pounding or grinding tuberous shapes between two stones. In fig. 52, the raw material lies in front of her and the processed food behind, while her large gathering bags lie beside her.

Women are often shown encamped together with all their possessions set around them in a careful catalogue. Five women sit

52 A woman pounds tubers or roots, the raw material in front of her and the prepared food behind her. Her bags are beside her and the curved line denotes her shelter. Murewa.

53 A group of women sit beside their sticks and bags. Mazowe.

54 *Gatherers whose equipment and adornments are shown in unusual detail. Harare.*

together, one apparently in the lap of another, with their sticks and tasselled bags in fig. 53. The five women and a child in fig. 55 have a greater number and variety of bags, some very large and formed of single skins with the legs hanging from them, some much smaller with a long looped handle. One also has a skin blanket. The seven women in fig. 56 relax, some sitting and others lying on their backs, with their children playing beside them, two with miniature bows and arrows. These women each have large bags with long curved protrusions, perhaps the spouts of water bags, and small triangular bags.

55 *Women encamped with all their possessions around them. Marondera.*

56 *A camp of women and children superimposed on an oval design. Marondera.*

57 *A detail from fig. 82. Seven couples lie on skin blankets and embrace, their weapons and possessions carefully catalogued beside them. Makonde.*

Parents, Families and Communities

Seven couples lie in close embrace in fig. 57, each couple on a large skin blanket, three with the slender figures of children beside them. Beside each family are its belongings: the bows and hunting bags filled with arrows of the fathers, long narrow bags with very long tassels hanging from the bottom and two flaps and a tuft sticking out of the tops; round shapes with long, thin, rigid and upright necks and small round spheres, both probably representing gourd containers. This painting is a particular *tour de force*, not only for its complexity, delicacy and detail but for the way that the artist, uniquely, has managed to tackle a new subject in a new way, to show objects one in front of another, using only one colour and shade of paint, by making the figures solid and hatching the blankets: a striking conceptual advance on almost all other paintings and a reminder that behind every painting is a particular individual with his own personal creative visual insight.

A whole community appears in camp in fig. 58. They are so carefully composed and grouped that one can identify five separate families – mother, father and one or two children, two childless couples and a single man. Once more the weapons and hunting bags of the men and the large collecting bags of the women lie beside their owners.

58 *A large group of several families encamped together. Mutoko.*

59 *A detailed scene of the people and their equipment in a large encampment. Bindura.*

Archetypes

The sample of paintings illustrated and discussed so far is typical of the great mass of paintings in Zimbabwe, and brings out many of the features of the art as a whole. It is clear that the art is highly selective in what could be depicted. People are shown in the prime of life and full health; no one is weak, wounded, sick, deformed, old or adolescent. Children, on the rare occasions that they appear, are almost always shown as miniature adults. The subsidiary activities of daily life are very seldom shown: sleeping, eating, playing, conversing, embracing, making love, rearing or feeding children, breaking or moving camp, making shelters, collecting firewood, preparing fires or cooking food, making or mending clothes, weapons, bags or other equipment, giving birth or suckling infants, tending the sick or mourning or burying the dead. Even hunters or gatherers are rarely engaged in the subsidiary activities that go with these roles: stalking, tracking, pursuing, attacking or killing their prey; butchering, transporting or sharing the spoils; digging out or collecting any of the great variety of possible plant foods; gathering firewood or drawing water.

People are not shown as individuals with recognisable features or any idiosyncrasies of body or behaviour. They exhibit no emotions, be it the tension of the stalk, the fears and excitements of the hunt or the weariness of walking long distances with heavy burdens. No one is laughing, joking, tearful, tired or hungry. There is no suggestion of the erotic. All other incidentals and distractions are as rigorously eliminated, including those of setting, landscape, weather, atmosphere, light or shade, heat or cold. The paintings are almost entirely unconcerned with the ephemeral, the topical or the incidental. In the vast majority of cases they do not illustrate specific events. This means they cannot be construed as narratives, be these historical records or personal anecdotes. They cannot and do not illustrate stories, myths or legends.

The paintings realise in the simplest and most easily legible ways a limited set of human archetypes, revealing the essence of the human condition, the basic roles of their society: man the hunter, woman the gatherer, the parent, family, band and community. They are visual generalisations, idealised constructs of the fundamental realities of the artists' society. They are simple and clear embodiments of mental concepts, depicted according to a specific and limited set of principles. The paintings both assert and celebrate the nature of society

60 *Different artists portray hunters, one with a quiver, and a single aproned woman raising her stick. Guruve.*

61 *An archetypal hunter. Northern Makonde.*

and the purpose of man on earth. They are pictorial realisations of an ideology, including of course, beliefs about man's creation, spiritual essence and power and destiny, in which the natural and supernatural worlds interpenetrate to form a single whole.

Archetypes are established through bodily forms, postures and gestures and through a simple shared set of signs, better known as attributes or emblems, which define basic social or economic roles. Bows and arrows, whisks, hunting bags, digging sticks and collecting bags are in essence emblems; so to a much lesser extent are the aprons, capes, gourds and blankets. It is relatively easy to identify these objects and interpret the qualities they represent. Others – like the lines and shapes on the head or penis – have no obvious reference to reality but it is already safe to assume that they too are emblematic.

Current popular interpretations – that the lines on the head illustrate a hunter's arrows inserted in a band tied round his head and ready for immediate use and that the attachments to the penis depict forms of multilation or adornment – are obviously mistaken. Lines on the head are found on men who are clearly not hunting and on women; even when on hunters, they are quite unlike their arrows in size and form. There is no other suggestion in traditions, history or archaeology that any pre-farming societies in Africa mutilated or adorned their penises. Such interpretations derive from the basic error that insists that the paintings are all direct illustrations of an external, visible reality and not distillations of conceptual constructs.

62 *A child suckles at its mother's breast. The father's weapons lie beside them. Mazowe.*

63 *The full equipment of a man and a woman and, perhaps, their food. Here possessions are used to signify people who are not themselves portrayed. Harare.*

Paintings and the San

How far then do the paintings show that they depict San people, that they are the work of San artists? The answer is obviously made difficult when the subject matter was so restricted and it was not the primary intention of the painters to depict physical features or daily life. They achieve this only indirectly and unintentionally. Nevertheless, the artists could only represent what they knew; their visual vocabulary had inevitably to draw on their experiences, however much these were filtered and distilled intellectually.

Physically, there is almost no indication that the humans had the small, stocky build or other physical or facial features that are generally associated with the San. The human subjects are on the contrary generally tall, lithe and slender, even unnaturally elongated. But this popular association of the San with particular physical characteristics is in any case largely false: known San exhibited a range of physiques and in remote times this was almost certainly even greater. The conventional image of the San relates only to some groups in recent periods who were in part at least the products of particular environments.

A few women do show the large buttocks and lumbar curvature that are generally considered characteristic of the San. But this is by no means generally true nor are such features emphasised. The erect penises painted on many men are also popularly considered to illustrate a characteristic peculiar to the San. This is not so. They are rather the product of an artistic convention that requires that every part of the body be shown clear of the remaining body outline. They are no more real than women's elongated breasts, erect and projecting from the body and placed one above the other.

64 *This page shows a selection of some of the very few paintings depicting everyday activities. Here a pot-bellied hunter eats the fruit from a heavily laden tree. Goromonzi.*

65 *Two hunters converse. Bindura.*

66 *A couple appear to make love. Wedza.*

The aprons, capes, large collecting bags and digging sticks in the paintings closely match the clothes and equipment of San women today. Some details reflect San customs with great precision: in the paintings women wear aprons over their buttocks much more commonly than at the front, an accurate reflection of San perceptions of the buttocks as the most erotic part of the body and hence the one part that must always be covered. No digging sticks are shown weighted with stones bored through the centre and wedged onto the sticks, a device generally associated with the San and the Later Stone Age. But this development was by no means general; rather it was devised to meet local conditions. The sizes of the families, hunting and gathering parties, camps and communities also match the social organisation of known San societies. But because the art was primarily concerned with establishing archetypes as economically as possible, using the minimum number of images to achieve this end, it is extremely dangerous to take the numbers of figures in any painted group as an indicator of actual social organisation.

The total absence of any convincing evidence that the painters were familiar with any of the features of African agricultural or pastoral communities places the paintings firmly in the Stone Age prior to the development of agriculture in the region over 2000 years ago. Occasional paintings do depict domesticated fat-tailed sheep; these help

67 *A figure wearing a tailed rear apron. Northern Makonde.*

68 *A woman with a cape made from the entire skin of a small animal slung over her back. Murewa.*

to confirm archaeological evidence in Zimbabwe that Stone Age peoples in parts of Zimbabwe had acquired sheep and were herding them about 2500 years ago. These paintings evidence at least some interest in new and alien animals. They strengthen rather than weaken the argument that the painters were never exposed to the changes that go with farming, such as village life, crops, cattle or metalworking.

There is one significant set of differences between the hunters in the paintings and the San. All San in historical times seem to have used small arrows with detachable heads on which poison was smeared and which lodged in the wounds of their prey while the shaft fell away. Archaeologists interpret many of the carefully shaped microlithic stone blades of the Later Stone Age as the barbs that were attached to similar composite arrows and also poisoned and there are strong analogies with known San equipment to support this. The arrows in the Zimbabwe paintings are quite different. These arrows are large, many have no separate heads and those that do have the heads firmly attached to the shafts with some sort of binding. There is no evidence in the paintings that microliths were made, used in arrows or hafted in wooden handles to form wood and leather working tools. These discrepancies suggest that either archaeologists are misinterpreting their material or that the paintings are even older than the full flowering of the Later Stone Age which shows such an overwhelming dependence on microliths to form the cutting and working edges of almost all weapons and tools.

69 *A man attacks a dog-like creature with a club. Mutoko.*

70 *Men, women and children in the abandoned, swaying postures of a dance. The women have white plumes on their heads, bangles on their wrists and tassels on their knees. White dots outline and adorn all the participants and flow from their bodies. For greater clarity, the colours are reproduced in reverse in this figure. Mutoko.*

3

DANCING AND TRANCING

San Practice

All San seem to have had a great number of different dances. Some were little more than children's games, some were spontaneous and purely for entertainment, while others were more highly disciplined, standardised and choreographed. Some were vehicles for individual feats of mimicry and acrobatics, or re-enacted dramatic events like hunts. Some were topical, invented by individuals and having only temporary popularity. In some communities women had their own dances from which men were excluded. Some dances, including dances to make rain, were the prerogative of old men. There were dances which were rituals to mark important thresholds in life; some of these took place very rarely – every five years or so.

The most important dance for all San was and is the healing or trance dance.[23] This takes place whenever it is considered propitious or necessary, when several bands have congregated close together, when there are tensions or worries within the community, when it is felt that people are alienated or 'sick', or when 'it feels right'. Trance dances can take place very frequently, perhaps every two or three days. They involve the whole community. Women gather wood and light a dance fire in an open cleared space in the centre of the camp. In the evening, when dancing starts, they sit together in a group close to the fire and clap the rhythm of the dance and sing. All can join in the dance – men, women and children – for longer or shorter periods. Participants dance in a line, in very close proximity and often in physical contact with each other, bending slightly forward and taking

71 *Figures with both arms and one leg raised in a more controlled dance posture than that shown in fig. 70. Goromonzi.*

short, pounding steps as they progress slowly round the fire. Some dancers hold their arms rigid; others raise and flutter theirs and swoop like a bird.

Very little equipment is necessary, and what there is, at least among the Kung today, is scarcely standardised. The only musical instruments used are rattles made of dried pods or other small containers with seeds or stones in them. These are attached to straps and tied round the ankles. Some dancers may wear a favourite hat or cap, perhaps with animal ears attached to it. Some carry a favourite walking stick and use it to support themselves as they stoop low during the dance. Others use two short dance sticks for the same purpose. Some may wave a fly whisk. Others tie animal tails over their buttocks.

As the dance progresses through the night, the atmosphere becomes highly charged. Excitement, tensions and emotions rise. The rhythm becomes more intense and compelling and the dancers' movements more violent. Those fully committed to trancing will dance together, supporting and encouraging each other and transmitting their rising potency between themselves. A few will then enter trance, stagger, collapse, fall and lie rigid or limp. All sweat profusely and some bleed from their noses. Others then gather round them, save them from injury, and lead them away from the dance circle. Here, with their spiritual energy or potency fully active, they are able to begin to heal.

They can now see with hypersensitive penetration into a patient's body, into the future and into far distances. As they diagnose a patient's ills, they will wrap themselves around him and rub him, using their blood and sweat – which are not just symptoms of their trance but potency itself. So they transmit something of their potency to the patient. They draw the patient's evils and sickness into themselves through intimate contact with him, sniffing and sucking at his body. Illness can be physically manifest as small sharp objects; these they will spit out and expel into the outer darkness, often with outspread arms and shrieks. Other trancers may leave their bodies, become transformed, enter or take on the bodily forms of animals, particularly lions and birds. In these forms they may prowl round and guard the camp or travel great distances to gain information about other groups, movements of game herds, or about centres of ripening edible plants or where rain clouds are gathering. They may enter the spirit world and there encounter spirits of the dead and the gods themselves and struggle with them for the lives of their patients and to overcome evils they have sent into the community.

During the trance dance, potency is everywhere – in the fire, the rhythms, the sounds, the name of the dance itself, the songs and steps.

72 To convey the violent action of this dance, the bodies of this couple have been strongly and unnaturally distorted. Mutoko.

Animals with a high degree of potency and spirits will gather in the dark on the outskirts of the dance as invisible participants. Potency is free, in the air itself. Like an electric charge, it can spark trance in the dancers, passing in a flash from one trancer to another.

Dance in the Paintings

An unusually large and coherent scene by a single artist is shown in fig. 73. It stands alone on the rock face. It includes at least seventy human figures with four additional figures and eleven antelope at the lower edge. The people have very little equipment and certainly no

73 *A uniquely large assemblage of several groups of people, amongst whom some women have taken off their aprons and children dance a little apart. Four men whirl in another dance on the left and below them clapping women provide the rhythm and chorus. Makonde.*

74 *Two lines of figures, almost every one of which holds a different object. The small figures that alternate with the larger may have been added later. Matobo.*

weapons and are not in files suggesting hunting or gathering parties. At the top a group of eleven large figures of women seem obviously to be dancing. Some hold hands and raise one leg, one crouches and raises her arms. Several have discarded their rear aprons which lie beside them, with two digging sticks. One waves her apron. On the upper left, a separate group of four men appear to be dancing by themselves and a lot more vigorously than the women, crouching, waving their arms and perhaps falling down. They also wave long thin whisks or have them attached to their arms. Below them sit seven figures, arms raised, fingers outstretched, apparently clapping, which is probably a dance chorus of women. In front of them is a formless blob, perhaps a dance fire, with three bags and some more figures sitting beside it, opposite the chorus. Moving right, there are more seated figures with their hands raised as if clapping – perhaps another chorus. One man with them waves a whisk. Below them are five men standing with arms raised and outstretched, perhaps engaged in a third dance.

Interpretation of this scene in terms of dancers and dance choruses seems reasonably firm, particularly as this complex panel contrasts sharply with two small scenes by the same artist on adjacent rocks, one of an archetypal hunting party and the other of an equally archetypal group of families encamped. In support, one can also use the detailed analogy between the group of women dancers, who have taken off their rear aprons, and San women who do the same in some of their dances from which men are excluded.[24] The postures and steps illustrated here – figures with raised legs and raised and outspread arms, figures in violent individual action, crouched figures, women waving their aprons or men waving their whisks – can be

75 *A line of men carrying a great variety of objects with others attached to the round swellings on their upper arms. Guruve.*

found in other paintings; but they are not common. Even less common, though they can be identified very occasionally, are figures which adopt the stances or equipment that identify dancers in the Drakensberg paintings: figures bent far forward and supporting themselves on short sticks, or holding their arms rigid and straight down behind their backs, or with masks. It seems there is no readily recognisable single archetype of the dancer in the Zimbabwe paintings, but rather that a variety of different forms and types of dance are represented.

In plate xxxv, seventeen figures, some walking along in a line and others in looser groupings, have their chests, stomachs and the insides of their arms and legs painted white. Some also have white circles round their eyes and two white stripes down their faces. These are the striking markings of sable antelope. The figures carry nothing. Bags, gourds, hides and other equipment and some seated figures are gathered around them, placing the scene in a camp. Two hold their arms rigid. These are the only indications that this is a painting of a dance. The body paint supports this and even enables us to interpret the scene as a Sable Dance.

Dancers were identified less by stance, posture or movement or by readily recognisable musical instruments than by a consistent range of objects that people held in their hands or tied – the straps are visible – to their bodies, especially to their arms or shoulders. Some are clearly whisks. Others I call discs, leaves, combs, crescents and flails: names that describe shapes rather than identify objects. These are now recognised as a fundamental characteristic of the art, but though many people have these emblems, they are seldom if ever shown in use in a scene illustrating a specific and identifiable activity,

76 *Figures leaning forward in a typical dance posture, their bodies partly obscured by the discs they all carry. They have no weapons but also carry a very varied range of other objects. Bindura.*

77 *A line of figures whose heads and bodies below the waist are obscured by tufted discs. Horned heads appear above the discs of some. Mazowe.*

and consequently they are extremely difficult to interpret. They do seem to be concrete or real objects and several look as if they may be musical instruments or plants. They may be simply emblems with only slight reference to reality. Certainly, whether they had any further function or not, they all served as emblems, intended to define more precisely and clearly, to their original audience, the nature of the people with whom they were associated. In many groups of people, every figure has or holds different objects of this sort, and often almost the entire range of emblems occurs within a single group of figures. A particularly dark, clear, skilled and detailed painting of a line of nine men is shown in fig. 75. This is no hunting party. The participants hold an array of different objects, including a bow, arrows of potency, whisks and flails (which are longer and thinner than the whisks). Leaves and discs are attached to small roundels on their upper arms.

In fig. 76 there are seventeen figures, some crouched with their legs raised in the posture of dancers, with their upper bodies obscured by discoidal shapes and their heads formed by two wide lobes, one on each side of the neck, and surmounted by a single curved plume. Most have small skin capes made of animal skins with the legs and tails still distinguishable hanging down their backs. They also have tails over their buttocks. One or two hold their discs and capes and make it clear that the discs are real objects, that all are holding them against their bodies and that the hand that holds them is hidden behind the disc. In the other hand each figure holds a different object. In one or two cases these are bows and arrows; in the remainder they are unidentifiable. The large discs have normally been taken to illustrate shields and thus the whole group has often been interpreted as the warriors of a Late Iron Age army observed by a San artist. Even allowing for the dating problems that this poses, it cannot be. Save for the discs, the figures are almost entirely unarmed. Their capes are a typical item of San women's clothing. Their inclined bodies and raised legs suggest more than anything that they are dancing.

Other examples of the use of similar discs have recently been identified. The thirteen figures in fig. 77 have three discoidal shapes on the bodies: one on each side of their heads and one over their waists. Antelope rather than human heads protrude above the discs of at least two. Tufts rise from the lower discs round their waists. Four carry bows and arrows and the remainder different objects. The figure on the extreme right bends down and holds a slightly curved line with a knobbed end in each hand, suggestive of dance sticks. The discs have finely furred or serrated edges suggesting something like feathers or bundles of grass rather than solid objects. In fig. 78 the four figures have furred discs over their heads with plumes rising from them. They have the postures of dancers. At least two wear capes and one an apron. One holds arrows and has a hunting bag in place of a cape, the others hold sticks. In fig. 79, the discs of the five main figures are deeply indented at the front and have tall broken plumes rising from them. Two wear rear aprons. One is fully armed and the others again carry different unidentifiable objects.

78 *Another group of figures with unidentifiable furred discs with furred edges from the same cave as fig. 77. Mazowe.*

These paintings are illustrated here not to affirm that they all represent dancers but to show some of the problems of interpretation. These paintings are all clearly similar, portray the same subject and were obviously intended to be very specific about what they illustrate. It is our understanding of them that is still faulty. The subjects are not warriors, nor are they hunters; their discs are neither shields nor forms of camouflage. To claim them as dancers is to some extent the result of a process of elimination. But one must be wary of making dance a compendium of all that is unidentifiable, of placing all problematic figures into the category of dancers simply because dance is the most likely activity or the only one we can envisage that brings together an array of objects being used outside their normal functions.

79 A third group of similar figures to those in figs 77 and 78, and from the same cave. Mazowe.

Trancers

Above the group of Sable Dancers in plate XXXII is a very large painting of a recumbent man. His face is once again painted with a sable's markings. He supports his head in one hand and holds up an oval object with the other. He rests the tip of one foot on the knee of his other leg very carefully and precisely. This is not the posture of a person who is asleep, unconscious, drunk or dead, nor is it necessarily the epitome of African indolence, which are the usual ways this image has been interpreted. He is not sprawled but carefully composed. His posture is explicit and makes it clear that he must be fully conscious, in control of his limbs even if unable to stand. This is, of course, a visual summary of the essential characteristics of a trancer in trance: unconscious to much of the world but fully conscious, even hyper-aware, in other realms.

At the very centre of fig. 73, and in some ways the visual focus of the whole composition, is another very similar figure, recumbent, his head in one hand, both knees raised, unable to stand but yet carefully composed. Both these images of recumbent figures are important components of dance scenes. These figures can therefore be taken as archetypes of trancers. Such figures are not common. Similar images can occur amidst ordinary camp scenes where there is little to suggest that the figures are doing anything but resting.

Few if any paintings show trancers engaged in their primary and most readily recognisable activity of healing – but this only reinforces the fact that it is characteristic of the art that few paintings depict any specific activities. In fig. 80 one figure is bending over another and touching the small of his back; both are bleeding profusely from their faces. These two figures suggest something of the intimate contact,

80 A detail from fig. 37. A man bends over and touches the small of the back of another crouched figure in a common San healing action. Both have 'tusks' rising from their faces and bleed profusely from their noses or mouths. Mutoko.

81 *The major part of a group of over thirty hunters who attack and flee from a large animal now no longer visible but marked by the line of arrows, top right, that once lodged in it. The four hunters at the top left were added by a later artist but have the same attributes as the originals. Mazowe.*

the massage and smearing of blood that are essential parts of the curing process. They are part of a panel of paintings which explore in metaphor and emblems many aspects of trance, as we shall see when we analyse the tusk-like emblems on the faces of these two figures, the elaborate heads of the hunters' arrows, the strange animals they shoot and the bird-like creature that hovers above them.

Sensations of Trancing

Studies of the Drakensberg paintings have made much of the ways that the physical sensations of trancing were expressed in the art. Paintings of dancers who are contorted, crouched and kneeling and with their hands on their chests or held rigidly behind their backs are interpreted as expressing reactions to the pains experienced on entering trance. Lines across the face illustrate the bleeding resulting from trancing. Elongated figures express the sensation of being stretched. Figures associated with fish or eels represent a common simile used to describe the sense of suffocation or drowning felt when trancing. Associations with birds represent a parallel metaphor for the sensation of floating or weightlessness. Lines rising from the head illustrate beliefs that the head is the point at which potency of trance enters the body or the spirit leaves it.

There are sufficient examples of similar images in the Zimbawe paintings to suggest that much the same verbal, visual and metaphoric vocabulary was recognised by the artists of Zimbabwe. But it seems to have been used very rarely; the examples that exist cannot be considered more than a very minor aspect of the art. Of the commoner features of the imagery, elongation can be interpreted as a universal characteristic of the style of the paintings as a whole rather than as the illustration of a particular sensation and attenuation can be seen as characterising not just trancers in trance but also a range of subjects inhabiting the spirit world, including spirits of the dead.

There are some strange features of the human imagery which may refer to some of the immediate physical consequences of trancing and which were used to situate particular images in a metaphysical realm. The line of figures interpreted as dancers in fig. 75 have roundels on their biceps and penises and pronounced semicircular swellings at the base of their necks. In fig. 81 a large company of energetic and agitated hunters, some with spears, aim their arrows towards the right and others flee in the opposite direction. They are all probably engaged in attacking a large animal that was once outlined and visible to the right; the only vestiges of it are a now isolated line of arrows that once pierced it. All have roundels inserted on their biceps and penises. Several have semicircular hoops on both sides of their necks, leading from the tops of their necks to their shoulders. At the top left smaller hunters, added to the composition later, have the same roundels and hoops showing that later artists fully understood the significance of these motifs to the scene. In fig. 82 another large group of finely detailed hunters surround the now badly damaged outline of another large animal, probably a rhino to judge by its legs. They too have roundels but these are on the biceps alone and they have no hoops on their necks. Lines have been left unpainted leading up the length of the bodies of some of them.

Roundels, neck swellings and hoops may depict the tensing, contraction and expansion of muscles and the dilation and throbbing of major veins, as the heart races with the excitement, fear and stress of a perilous hunt or the climax of a trance dance. As we shall see,

82 *The best preserved of the hunters who once surrounded a large outlined rhinoceros. A small rhinoceros, its belly pierced by three arrows, is placed under the large animal in echo of it. Makonde.*

77

83 *The main interest in this panel is focused on the six figures between the antelope at the right edge, who appear to be progressively transforming into bird-like creatures. Hunters sharing much of their character have been painted by the same artist at the left edge. Marondera.*

depictions of the hunting of particularly large and dangerous animals was used in the art as a key metaphor for trancing, possibly in part because the sensations experienced in both were so similar. The unpainted lines running up the bodies suggest the channels up which the San believe potency flows and rises at the climax of trance.

In both figs 81 and 82 there are single figures which, though painted by the same artists, as carefully as the others, sharing many of their features and being integral parts of the original compositions, have deliberately been left incomplete. In fig. 81 a figure on the left has no arms or lower legs. In a figure bending forward in fig. 82 the whole of the body above the waist has been reduced to the narrow line of the spine. The visible incompleteness and losses shown in these two examples may have sought to express something of other aspects of sensations that trancers say they experience in trancing.

Certainly carefully painted figures that were nevertheless deliberately left incomplete had an important role in the art. This was more than simply to indicate people suffering one of the sensations of trance. It served to remind anyone who saw them that every scene, every activity, every group of people had within it elements from beyond the natural world: that a world of potency, spirits and gods impinged on and permeated every human circumstance. Like the carefully composed figure of a trancer, these images immediately introduced a new dimension, a new level of comprehension and significance to any composition in which they were placed.

Transformations

Trancers are believed to take on the bodily forms of some animals when they seek to travel out of their bodies, to enter the spirit world. They can then also assume characteristics of the animal species they inhabit. With the swiftness of a bird's flight, the strength and ferocity of a lion, they may travel great distances fast and effortlessly, see what is far away, protect their communities against all dangers and do battle with evil. There are in Zimbabwe some images and scenes of people that appear to be in the process of such transformations. They are rare but dramatic. Of the six figures on the right centre of fig. 83, the four lowest are clearly basically human although their limbs are particularly long and bony, their legs end in swellings like bone ends rather than feet and their hands have two or three long fingers like talons. Their necks are inordinately long, their heads misshapen, with linear projections from their faces and lines like plumage rising from their heads. One has a huge, gaping beak-like mouth. All have a long line ending in a tuft – like that otherwise associated with the penis –

84 *An isolated painting of a single hunter, unsual in the four hoops that come from his neck and in the depiction of his scrotum. Makonde.*

emerging directly from the navel or abdomen. The two figures just above these four are clearly part of the same group and have the same plumage and gaping beaks. But now, the one on the right lies on its back, its arms have turned into wings and its back seems to be covered in fur or short ruffled feathers. The one on the left is now clearly a bird, with a wing raised, a long thin neck and beak, enlarged knees and long legs that end in definite bird's talons though they are still very like the fingers of the other figures. Scattered among the same panel of paintings are at least six other figures that are clearly part of this group: some have bows, arrows and shoulder bags but all also have the long necks, protruding or gaping mouths and tufted lines from their abdomens. Their agitated movements and waving arms carry some suggestion of a bird's flight. More clearly and unambiguously than in any other set of paintings, these figures seem to illustrate, almost in a narrative sequence, stages in the transformation of people to birds. Once this is recognised, many more otherwise puzzling paintings can be associated with this imagery.

The creatures along the elephant's back in fig. 85 carry the same connotations. Neither the males nor females have plumage or beaks but they have long thin limbs, the lower parts painted white, and long talon-like fingers. They lie on their backs, wave their arms or move along on their hands and legs. One, shown in fig. 11, seems to be partly covered in feathers. Among them is one creature with bird's wings outspread but a head that is much more human than bird-like. Beside it is a much more complete bird with a plump body and long leg, neck and beak.

In fig. 86 a similar creature with outspread wings hovers close to the healer of fig. 80 and above two hunters, one with a spear of potency and the other aiming an arrow of potency, about to despatch a zebra whose lowered head shows that it is already dying. The winged creature has a human head and single human leg. A much larger, more careful and detailed painting, fig. 87, shows three of these composite creatures that are part bird and part human. They have the bodies, penises, legs and feet of men and hurry along with a human gait but their outstretched arms have become elaborately feathered wings. Their heads and especially the bosses of their foreheads are grossly enlarged but they have human faces as well as huge curved horns. By such means, the artist sought to emphasise beyond doubt the alarming extraordinariness, the grotesque and frightening nature of these creatures. Much less alarming winged human figures are shown in figs 88 and 91. Both are one-legged and both have clear, carefully painted and detailed feathers on their wings. This leaves no doubt about what the artists intended or what the images depict. The grotesque nature attributed to bird-like creatures is clear in the very

85 *A detail from fig. 11, showing crouched and recumbent human figures with stick-like limbs and long talons in different colours. Two quite different and even more bird-like creatures are among them. Wedza.*

86 *A detail from fig. 37. A winged creature hovers above a hunter and his dying victim. Mutoko.*

87 *Three monstrous horned and winged creatures. Harare.*

88 *The one-legged figure has feathered arms or wings and bleeds from his face. Guruve.*

careful little painting, fig. 89. This creature has no human features and is particularly far removed from almost any reference to the natural world. More than any other it is an entirely imaginative visual image demonstrating the delight the artist took in the complexity and pattern of line for its own sake. But there can be little doubt that it is also another exploration and representation of a mystery of the supernatural closely allied to those already described.

In fig. 90 there are eight monstrous figures, their heads misshapen and set directly on their shoulders, without necks, their mouths gaping wide and straining upwards, toothless but for two long, curved, rodent-like incisors or fangs rising from their lower jaws, their legs swollen and their feet reduced to pegs rather than hooves. Tufted lines come from their penises. They hold a varied range of objects like some dancers we have already examined: a leaf shape, comb shapes and, in one case, a bird and small animal. A ninth figure, the most fearsome of all, has a long tail and bristling hair covering his body, suggesting that he has entered the final and fullest form of transformation here, into a feline – though he also seems to have long misshapen horns that are unlike those of any known antelope. More than any others, these figures suggest something of the horror that the San associate with the spirit world.

Conclusions

This chapter contains what appear to be some of the most directly illustrative images in the art. The large panel of figures by a single artist, fig. 73, seems clearly to illustrate several activities that are essential characteristics associated with the periodic congregation of different groups: male and female dances, the clapping chorus, the dance fire, the onlookers and a trancer. Plate xxxv includes considerable careful detail of the body paint with which dancers adorned themselves and signified their associations with the animal whose potency permeated a particular dance. In its depiction of men changing into birds, fig. 83 can be read as a record of progressive stages in transformations, making it the nearest thing in the art to a narrative painting. Dances are illustrated through straightforward and realistic descriptions of a wide range of what seem to be characteristic accessories that dancers wear and carry and that may also define the specific type of dance that is being performed. Trancers have few if any supernatural trappings. They seem to have been illustrated with almost the same directness as dancers but their characteristic posture

89 *A tiny, idiosyncratic creation of an artist delighting in linear complexity and conveying the unreality of some winged creatures. Guruve.*

90 *Fearsome creatures with gaping mouths, two tusk-like teeth and no feet. In the centre, one is also horned, tailed and covered in fur. Harare.*

91 *Another one-legged man with wings replacing his arms. Mazowe.*

is an artificial and careful construct designed to convey, economically, clearly and legibly, the essence of trance: physical weakness combined with extreme awareness. Mental control is exemplified by the careful placing of the legs and hands holding the head, loss of physical control by the recumbent posture. The wide use of this posture demonstrates how the art, through a very explicit and restricted vocabulary of forms and stylised constructions achieved comprehension by its audience. This was reinforced through juxtapositions of images with other images denoting potency.

Symbol and metaphor were used in much richer and more varied ways. The Zimbabwe art was more concerned with the deeper realities, more fundamental aspects of belief, and profounder ramifications of the actions of potency, than has previously been thought.

4

THE IMAGERY OF POTENCY

The San and Potency

As far as historical records and anthropological studies go, they all agree that every known San group appears to have shared a common belief that all people have within themselves an individual, innate, personal spiritual energy or power. This has been studied most fully among the Kung San, who know their potency as *num*. It is a real, material substance, visible and tangible to trancers. A trancer's sweat, for instance, is not seen as a physical consequence of trance, but as potency itself made manifest. A person's potency resides in his *gebesi*, the abdomen between diaphragm and waist and especially in the liver and spleen.[25]

The activation of potency is a fearful thing. When it is active, potency induces painful sensations of tingling and prickling, of cramped, bunched and stretched muscles, of distended, drumming veins, of nausea and retching, and of suffocation akin to drowning. Active potency causes trance, some loss of consciousness and a danger of burning or injury as the trancer stumbles about near the dance fire. Trance is believed to be not just similar to death but a form of death itself. The trancer enters the domain of spirits and gods, a dangerous, frightening, foul and evil-smelling place, where the trancer is threatened and at grave risk from the fearful, death-dealing and immensely powerful potencies of spirits and gods. Few therefore choose to cultivate their ability to make their potency active – among the Kung perhaps one man in three and one woman in ten.

An individual's potency is activated not just by his own efforts but

92 *A man with a distended abdomen and with whisks tied to both his shoulders. Bindura.*

93 *The large figure of a man with a grossly distended body and holding up a comb in each hand. Goromonzi.*

94 *A woman with a distended body carrying a leaf shape and stick. Marondera.*

95 *A woman with a distended abdomen holds up a leaf and has combs tied to both shoulders. Mutoko.*

96 *Another woman, with very similar devices to that in fig. 95. Mutoko.*

through the support of the community as a whole, by the potency inherent in the songs, rhythms and clapping of the trance dance, in the dance steps and in the dance fire round which the dancers circle. Trancers are also encouraged and supported by each other. It is believed that experienced trancers can transmit potency during the dance to those new to the experiences, but who seek to join them in trance, by shooting small, invisible, magical arrows of potency into their bodies.

As it becomes active in the *gebesi*, potency swells, 'boils', 'boils over', 'bursts open' and rises through the 'channels' of the body. It then gives the trancer power to heal those in any form of social or physical distress, to transform himself and to take the forms of animals and birds. It enables him to release his spirit to go forth and gain knowledge of and influence other communities, animals, rain, the whole material and spiritual world. All this is done through the trancer's community, for its sake and for its good.

How much of this, the fundamental core of all San belief, spiritual life and practice, is evidenced in the paintings? Many correlations between isolated individual images and aspects of potency can be made. These are often no more than mere 'games of ethnographic snap' and prove nothing. They too often assume that each image is a cypher in a code and that ethnographic correlates break this code. On the other hand, through sustained comparative analyses, many different defined aspects of the imagery can be consistently correlated with many different aspects of belief. When motifs and images can be identified, when the ways that they are placed and embedded in different contexts can be distinguished, when they can be shown to move across a large spectrum of belief, when the same defined forms, which presumably carry similar content, can be recognised in their different conjunctures, these associations and relationships can refine our understanding of both form and content.

It is a building process. We must therefore suspend judgement on the merits of the process until the building is finished, the analysis complete, all the relevant imagery fitted into place and its pervasive coherence demonstrated and apparent. One may then be on ground sufficiently firm to make forays into areas of belief that no longer survive in any record but the paintings. If this carries conviction, we can have some assurance that the interpretations carry validity, that some of the significant elements of prehistoric beliefs are firmly in place, even if the full story can never be fully revealed.

Distended Figures

There are recurrent paintings of men and women standing or walking, sometimes in pairs, who have swollen abdomens. Often lines emerge directly from their abdomens. Much more striking are distinctive sets of paintings, perhaps limited to the north or west of Zimbabwe, almost all of women, and generally in pairs, who are remarkable for their grossly swollen abdomens. They face forward with their heads turned sideways and stand with their legs bent and apart and their arms spread wide apart, bent at the elbows and raised, in a position that matches that of their legs. They have distinctive sets of objects in their hands or tied to their upper arms or shoulders, shaped like 'leaves', 'crescents' or 'combs'. The latter are triangular shapes atop a thin shaft or handle and serrated round the edges. Whatever they may represent and whether they have any correspondence to real objects or have more abstract connotations, they can be taken to signify particular qualities, as emblems that served to define these distended figures more precisely. These qualities were complex and important for no other figures have so many such signs associated with them and one – the crescent – is only found in the hands of these figures.

These figures have generally been interpreted as pregnant and hence as symbols of fertility, 'earth mothers', or 'mother goddesses'. This cannot be. Not only is there at least one painting of a man with exactly the same stance, attributes and abdominal swelling but the shape of the swellings is not that of the womb of a pregnant woman. The womb is positioned higher up the body, is smaller, firmer and does not extend round the sides of the body. These swellings are much larger, lower on the body, and sag towards the bottom. It is the

97 Small malformed figures attached to lines emerging from a distended figure with a painted body, antelope ears and an extended muzzle, holding up a comb. The left side of this figure is damaged by exfoliation. Wedza.

98 *Lines, from a distended female figure holding a crescent, curve across a panel of paintings. She has a small partner, in the same posture as herself, beside her. Mutoko.*

99 *(opposite) A distended female figure holding combs is painted over one of a group of trees. Arrow shapes have been painted over the lines that come from her enlarged genitalia. Goromonzi.*

sides of the body that exhibit the distension not the front. The whole of the abdomen is enlarged, not just the womb. The artists were careful observers and accurate recorders and were aided in this by all the principles of legibility that define their art. If they had intended to represent pregnancy, they would have painted the mother in profile to show clearly the outline of the womb swollen at the front of her body. Here, unusually in the art, the figures are shown from the front, a position in which the swollen womb would not break the outline of the body. These are not mistakes of observation, loose or careless choices of viewpoint: the art is too conventional to allow for that. This detailed formal analysis thus makes it clear that it is precisely the part of the body that the Kung call the *gebesi* that is distended. The *gebesi* swells when the potency of which it is the container becomes active. Thus these figures are archetypes of potency that is active and 'boiling' and hence perhaps a particular category of particularly potent trancers or healers.

Lines emerge from between the legs of some of these distended female figures, sometimes from enlarged vulvae. Where a pair of figures is shown, invariably only one generates such lines. Often in stripes of more than one colour, the lines can meander or zig-zag for considerable distances across the rock surface, over earlier paintings and with other paintings superimposed on them. These lines cannot, as is popularly believed, represent the waters of childbirth. They are too carefully painted, their forms so similar, so controlled, so exactly delineated, their stripes – often of different colours – so carefully separated, that they cannot represent a fluid. This is confirmed if these lines are compared with the ways that fluids like sweat or blood were represented – by formless streams of flecks or the simplest, short straight lines. Some of these complex zig-zag lines also have careful spikes or hooks painted at their angles which is not something associated with a fluid. And in at least one example, fig. 155, identical lines rise from the abdominal area of a recumbent male figure, the archetypal trancer. The lines were deliberately given their distinctive characteristics so that they might retain their own identity, significance or meaning even when their usual source – the distended figure – was dispensed with or reduced to the simplest blot of paint (as in fig. 100). They are thus another emblem. These lines must represent the particular form of potency generally associated with that contained and activated by the distended figures and released from their swollen *gebesi*.

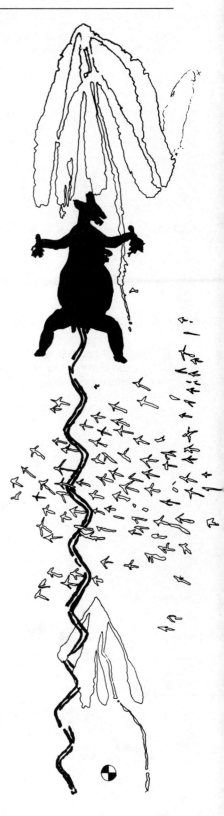

100 *A line, to which a malformed figure is attached, rises from a circular shape. Wedza.*

101 *Another distended woman holds a crescent aloft. Flecks flow from her armpit and abdomen. A bleeding figure crawls along one of the lines coming from her. Mutoko.*

Oval Designs

The distended figures are the most directly illustrative representations of aspects of potency in the art of Zimbabwe, but they are a
comparatively minor part of the exploration of this subject. The most
important representations of potency introduce a complex degree of
symbolism to the subject as they penetrate its spiritual or metaphysical content. They are much more numerous, colourful and complex
than anything described so far. No one can deny that they seem
puzzling, even impenetrable, but penetrate them we must for they
are clearly the most significant set of images in the art of Zimbabwe.
They provide the test against which all interpretation of the art
ultimately rests. We get little help from research in other parts of
southern Africa for they are entirely limited to Zimbabwe.

These designs look abstract. Their basic forms and compositions
are simple, even geometric, based on comparatively simple clusters
of oval shapes. The usual interpretation of ovals used to be that they
illustrated the granite boulders and hills that are such a distinctive
feature of the Zimbabwe landscape and thus form the only known
San landscape painting. Variations on this saw them as distant views
of cultivated fields, villages or clouds. These sorts of interpretation
are not quite dead. One archaeologist, accepting apparently without
question that ovals represent striking elements of landscape, has
recently played another game of ethnographic snap with them, relat-
ing them to San concepts of territoriality and ways they denoted this.

Currently, the most popular interpretation of the designs sees them
as illustrating bees' nests. The outlines are hollow bark hives, the
cores are combs, the dots are larvae and the arrowheads are the
insects themselves. This is given significance by using ethnographic
evidence that some San believe that bees and honey are sources of a
particularly powerful potency. This interpretation originates
through identifying the Zimbabwe designs with six paintings in a
Drakensberg gorge where somewhat similar shapes have bees
painted in some detail beside them or are approached by people
apparently 'climbing ladders' – 'honey gatherers'. Nothing like these
is associated with the Zimbabwe designs. Ladder-like designs in
Zimbabwe are clearly aggregations of flecks and have the same
connotations as the lines emanating from distended figures. The
comparison between details of the designs in the two regions is
tenuous and unconvincing and takes no account of the great variations in the Zimbabwe designs. All the popular interpretations are
still firmly based on an insistence that all paintings are directly
illustrative. For this reason alone, I find them all deeply suspect.

Many find the most complex of the oval designs very beautiful. As

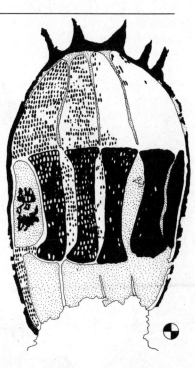

*102 A rigidly composed oval design
with dark cores topped with white
caps and both covered in lines of
dots in contrasting colours.
Guruve.*

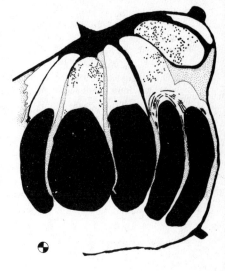

*103 A more fluidly designed
composition, with the shapes of the
ovals adjusted to fit within the
enclosing line. Guruve.*

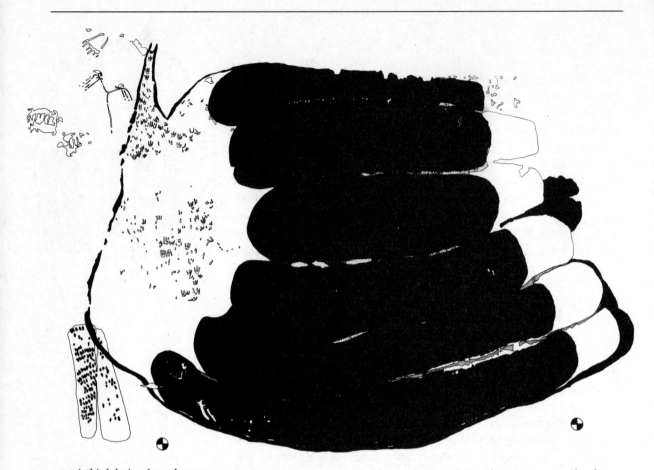

104 *A third design from the same site as figs 102 and 103. White arrow shapes flow down the orifice in the enclosing line and fill the spaces between the ovals. Two white birds perch on a tree beside the opening. The design is superimposed on a simpler version of the design: two ovals covered in lines of dark dots. Guruve.*

a consequence some, in desperation, claim they were purely decorative, intended to do no more than beautify the artists' surroundings, no more than a 'wallpaper'. This cannot be. Their basic forms are too consistent. It is difficult to imagine undisciplined and meaningless decoration restricting itself to a single set of motifs or following such rigid principles. And there are no indications elsewhere in the art that any of the imagery was primarily or even significantly decorative. The focus on content is so self-evident in all the other imagery that it must logically be extended to these designs also.

It will be shown instead that these are not abstract paintings but sophisticated abstractions of ideas and beliefs about potency. They are mental constructs developed to realise visually what is very largely invisible. They are distillations, once more reducing the incidental to focus on the essence. They, more than any other paintings, are symbols containing multiple visual allusions difficult to define in words and many of which we no doubt fail to recognise, let alone comprehend.

In its most complete and characteristic form, an oval design has dark oval or rectangular cores, often of different colours, standing

close together in a line or lying horizontally one above the other. Often the cores are of different sizes and their shapes are curved so that they fit into a more or less circular space. They may be enclosed in the outline of a circle, sometimes with spikes attached to the outside of it and with a single opening breaking it. The dark cores are often given white semicircular caps at one or both ends. They are also covered with very regular lines of carefully painted white dots. The interstices between the cores and the spaces between them and the enclosing circle are, in the most complex examples, filled with small white motifs painted with three strokes of the brush, and resembling birds on the wing, a bird's footprint or our convention for an arrowhead. They point in every direction and some emerge from the orifice in the circle. In a simple variant, the spiked enclosing circle remains but the ovals are omitted and the interior completely filled with simple flecks of paint, which again flow out of an opening.

Oval designs can take a great variety of forms. Some remind us of organic plant forms: some even have tufts apparently growing from multiple enclosing lines. Others are more rigidly organised, symmetrical and geometric. Some have a rich range of differently coloured cores and great care was taken in their white detailing and embellishment. In many only a single colour now survives. The simplest are no more than one or two small, dark, semi-rectangular shapes. In figs 110 and 111 it is difficult to be certain whether these small paintings represent elements of an oval design or a section through a fruit and its seeds. The dark cores covered with white dots can become a chequer board in a single colour with each core made up of squares of solid colour alternating with squares consisting just of the dots. Some reproduce only the dots and enclose these in lines

106 *An even smaller and simpler design, dots painted between two lines, was painted on the same rock face as fig. 105. Murewa.*

107 *A very large design based on successive lines of the cusps of the caps of ovals. Mazowe.*

representing the core; others replace the lines of dots with grids of white lines. Some ovals have caps that are darker than the cores. Smaller ovals often cluster near the openings of the enclosing circles. Some openings were extended to form a narrow, carefully painted and elaborated orifice, particularly reminiscent of the neck of a stomach. In many the shapes of the outer cores were adjusted to fit into an overall shape or to fit round ovals that were painted earlier. Some designs were partly repainted and renewed with fresh white dots, caps and outlines. Some compositions were complete in themselves and self-contained from the start; others were continually added to, to provide an expanding field for new paintings placed over them.

108 *A dark core and light cap enclosed by multiple lines which come together as a tuft at one end. Mutoko.*

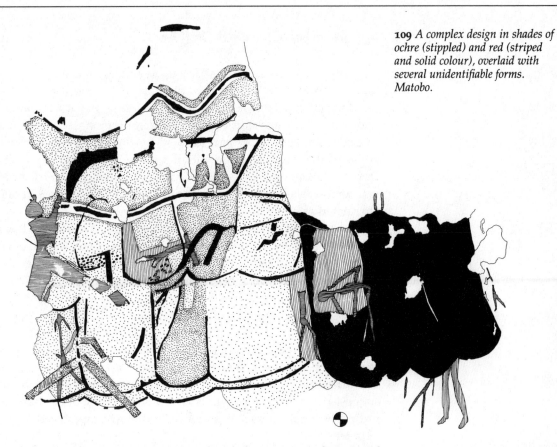

109 *A complex design in shades of ochre (stippled) and red (striped and solid colour), overlaid with several unidentifiable forms. Matobo.*

Some emphasise the rounded caps of the cores to the virtual exclusion of all else: fig. 107 is a very large painting, now little more than a dark stain, isolated on the almost horizontal overhang of a deep shelter. It seems at first a particularly crude, formless and meaningless meander. More careful consideration and comparison with other paintings reveal that it is built up of successive lines of cusps of ovals, in five rows, one above the other, some separated by lines, the most prominent of which follows the curves of the largest set of cusps.

110 *(far left) A very small and unidentifiable shape within a circle formed by two lines. Mazowe.*

111 *(left) Comparatively large dots fill a tiny circular shape, like the seeds of a fruit. Guruve.*

Interpretation of the Oval Designs

The range of forms of the oval designs is enough in itself to suggest that we are dealing with representations of a concept or a set of interlocking concepts, none of which has easy visual equivalents. They carry a range of allusions, place different emphases on different components. They allow part to stand for the whole. They are creations of the mind, working within a set of beliefs and expressing these within an established visual tradition, canon and rules of representation. They are not recreations of things seen and retain only attenuated references to the visible, tangible world.

A very simplified interpretation of these designs can be made but one that may have a certain validity for it accounts for almost every element of the designs within a single coherent explanation that accords with known San beliefs about potency. The enclosing circle represents the abdominal wall, the spikes arrows of potency lodged in it or the pricking sensations associated with the activation of potency. The ovals represent the internal abdominal organs, including the main sources of potency, the liver and spleen. The ordered lines of dots suggest potency latent in the abdomen and its organs. The arrow or bird shapes and flecks escaping through the orifice suggest potency in an active form, 'boiling', 'rising', and 'bursting forth'. The whole is thus a representation of the Kung *gebesi*, the fount of potency.

112 *A recumbent trancer, surrounded by the heads of oribi, has a rectangle carefully left unpainted on his chest. The oval design below him has a similar unpainted rectangle in it, apparently deliberately signifying an identity between the two images. Harare.*

XIV *(opposite) A close-up of two figures suggesting trance-dancing. One waves fly whisks and has decorative tufts and a 'disc-shaped' emblem on his upper arms. The other is recumbent and holds a long pipe or rod. Murewa.*

xv (left) Superpositioning can be extremely dense, even at small sites. Detail of part of this panel is disentangled in fig. 31. Marondera.

xvi (opposite) A wealth of white body decoration adorns two archetypal hunters. The intricacy of detail is all the more astonishing for these paintings are 5m above the ground and little can be seen from below. They are reproduced again superimposed on the elephant at the bottom right corner of the front endpapers. Bindura.

XVII (above) *A line of men, also shown in fig. 75, hold a variety of emblems, including 'flails' and 'magic arrows'. Further emblems, 'leaves' and 'combs', are attached to their shoulders. Guruve.*

XVIII (below) *A line of hunters in a distinctive style, either by one artist or a small regional school. They are distinguishable by the mass of detail, long thighs, low knees and bulging calves. The outlined head and foreleg of a very large crocodile viewed from below is in the top right corner. Harare.*

XIX (above) An unusually simple pair of distended figures, with legs apart and one holding the distinctive 'crescent' shape only found with such people. Mutoko.

XX (below) Another pair of distended figures, outlined in ochre and ornamented with armlets, necklaces and girdles in white. The lines emerging from the left figure have one-legged figures attached to them, shown in fig. 129. Mutoko.

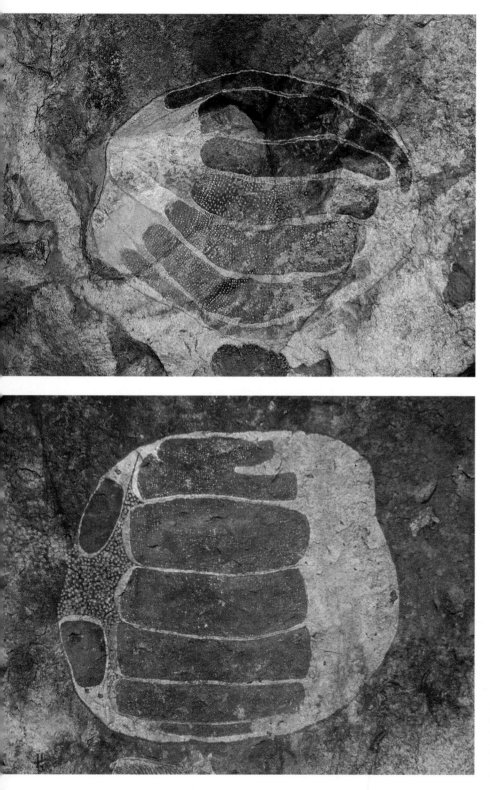

XXI *The key symbol in Zimbabwean paintings: dark cores capped and embellished in white to form a series of oval shapes fitted within an enclosing line. 'Arrow' shapes emerge from an opening on the right of the oval: they are shown in detail in fig. 121 and discussed there. Mazowe.*

XXII *A well-preserved oval design on the same cave wall as the paintings in plate XXVIII. 'Arrow' shapes enter and emerge from the opening on the left. Guruve.*

XXIII *(above) Oval designs are the only paintings positioned to take advantage of irregularities in the rock surface. Here the cores covered in white dots have been carefully placed and adjusted to cover the dark boss of an alien rock inclusion in the granite. Part of the same panel as plate* XXI. *Mazowe.*

XXIV *(below) The largest and most beautiful of all the oval designs. The white caps are delicately coloured and separated to suggest an infinite recession of nested ovals: the summation of the potency of a whole community. Two darker ovals with semi-human creatures between them have been added, top left. Matobo.*

xxv *Three of many extremely elongated figures in a cave dominated by a painting of a lion hunt. This association and their powerful hunched shoulders, small heads, fur, long claw-like fingers and feline tails suggest that they personify San beliefs about transformations of trancers into lion spirits or of lions taking invisible semi-human forms. Matobo.*

A more remote and generalised explanation, but one that is equally congruent with the more direct and literal interpretation just outlined, is that the clusters of ovals represent the community of trancers, their individuality and identity submerged in a single unified social whole, each replete with potency and together generating and releasing a stream of potent energy. The circular outline thus bounds and defines an entire potent community.

It is even possible to retain the interpretation that the oval designs might in some sense represent beehives as a source of a particularly powerful potency. This does not deny my interpretations. It can be accepted as another reading of the multiple allusions of the designs. But it is simplistic, minimising or denying the rich symbolic content of the designs and reductive in its emphasis on a narrow illustrative aspect.

Despite my attempts at a formal analysis and then an interpretation of the designs by themselves, there is clearly little in the visual elements of the oval designs to suggest directly and unambiguously that they represent or refer to some form of human potency. This interpretation is derived much more certainly from a consideration of their associations. Plates XXXII and XXXIII show one of the finest and best preserved single paintings in Zimbabwe, retaining its mass of detail in full. It is of a recumbent trancer, his face painted with the markings of a sable antelope and his body covered in lines of white dots like the core of an oval. A single dark oval core covered in identical dots is attached to the small of his back, in fact to his *gebesi*. This arrangement emphasises a close physical relationship between a trancer's *gebesi* and an unmistakable oval. It is clear that the trancer must in some sense be identified with the oval. The two share the same qualities. A smaller, simpler and somewhat damaged figure below him confirms this. He adopts the same posture as the large figure and much of his body is covered with a set of ovals. There are other paintings in which the body of a figure seems to consist of forms derived from the oval designs. In other trancers, areas of the body and specifically the *gebesi* have been left unpainted and given the shape of an oval and ovals have been placed beside their abdomens, once more emphasising an equivalence between the oval and the body or abdomen of humans and particularly trancers. One painting of a trancer has a strange rectangle carefully left unpainted on his abdomen. An oval beneath him has a blank area in exactly the same shape incorporated in it. These two identical rectangles on two different but adjacent images seem to have been intended to serve as a sign establishing a relationship between the two, a shared identity.

113 *An oval shape forms a man's body through the addition of rudimentary limbs and head and a tufted emblem indicating his penis. Harare.*

114 *A recumbent hunter or trancer, his abdomen left unpainted and with an area of paint matching the same oval shape placed beside him, comparable to plate XXXII. Murewa.*

115 *Flecks appear to emerge from the rectangular shape held by one man and surround two branched forms. Goromonzi.*

Dots and Flecks

We have already seen how the dots on the dark cores of ovals can be transformed into flecks and flow out of the circles enclosing the ovals. The relationship between flecks and ovals is reiterated in a different and idiosyncratic way in a painting where flecks within a much larger field of flecks are so patterned that they aggregate and cohere into a clearly recognizable oval: the flecks are so painted that they reconstitute their origin, the oval shape.

In fig. 115 flecks appear to be generated not by ovals but by a more directly and obviously human source. Several strange figures have long slab-like torsos, long thin muzzle-like faces, a variety of emblems attached to them or held in their hands and, in the case of men, long thin lines ending in a small tuft in place of their penises. One man holds out a long rectangle or cylinder from which flecks flow down and surround three tree-like forms, the smallest with visible roots and the largest with trunk and branches.

The association of flecks with trees is so common that it can be taken as characteristic of the Zimbabwe paintings. One of the small-

116 *The flecks at the top are painted in the form of an oval. The attenuated figure with large ears is matched by two tiny figures in fig. 115. Marondera.*

est, simplest and clearest illustrations of this is fig. 119. In fig. 118 the field of flecks is much larger but again centred around tree forms with roots, trunks and branches. In fig. 117 some of the flecks are painted in lines and seem to flow and have direction. They are also attached to tree forms so that they seem to form the leaves, though they also

117 *Flecks formed into long lines and clustered on branched forms. Top left they form a grid or 'ladder' along which malformed semi-human creatures crawl. Makonde.*

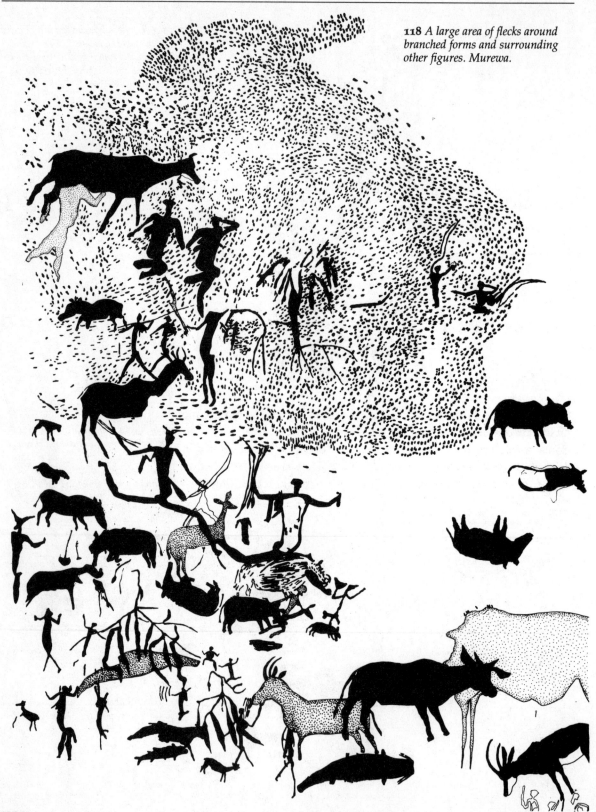

118 *A large area of flecks around branched forms and surrounding other figures. Murewa.*

cluster in the same way down the lines that represent the tree trunks. The same is true of fig. 119. In many painted panels flecks round trees cover very large areas, sometimes stretching across entire cave walls. The association of flecks with trees led earlier authorities to claim that they were the most important demonstration of landscape painting distinctive to the art in Zimbabwe and that flecks represented grass, grasslands, bushveld, streams or lakes.

That arrowheads may have been active agents in the transformation of the plant world is suggested by fig. 121. Two oval designs do not contain or generate flecks or arrowheads but have their openings facing towards each other. The only area of well-preserved paintings between them shows white arrowhead shapes clustered round plant forms. These are strange and unnatural. Each stem has two or three large leaves or flowers. As these separate from their stems they take on the forms of ovals and each has a distinctive white cap otherwise only found on ovals. In this painting natural forms are being transformed through their association with arrowheads to become ovals; they are both made potent by the potency represented by flecks and arrowheads and are themselves sources of potency.

The same can be said of fig. 120. The flecks and trees may well have been painted by one artist and the human figures by others. This does not negate an intentional association. It is the twenty-five to thirty small figures along the top, some of them now fragmentary, that are of particular interest here. They are simple, sexless, without any weapons or other equipment, and form no composition suggesting

119 *Flecks entirely surround a small painting of a tree. Marondera.*

120 *Flecks again form lines and cluster like leaves on trees. Along the top, semi-human figures with long drooping necks and heads reminiscent of the plants in fig. 121 echo the forms of the 'trees'. Mazowe.*

122 *(opposite below) Flecks both cluster as leaves on a 'tree' and along the outlines of strange creatures with only one fore- and one hind-leg. Many of the human figures, by different artists, seem to be dancers; some have distorted arms and the largest arches his back in an impossible way. Makonde.*

any joint action. Most have very long drooping necks, swelling gradually and surmounted by 'drop-shaped' heads. These heads and necks are sufficiently reminiscent of the plant shapes in fig. 121 to suggest that the same sorts of influences are being transmitted and that the same sort of transformation is taking place in both.

Clusters of flecks, because of their connotations with potency and particularly the release of active, powerful and dangerous potency, were used to point to the heightened significance of some of the imagery, to the presence of potency, of supernatural power, inherent in a situation. Dots and flecks can be interpreted on at least two different 'levels'. In representational terms, according to their contexts, they may stand for beads, blood, sweat, perhaps birds and, less probably, bees. We have already seen that all symbols in the paintings have references, often multiple, to the visible world of the artists and their audiences. But the underlying content of this variety is the same: potency. This is generated in the oval designs. It flows across large areas of paintings and affects many diverse subjects. It can cluster, coalesce and congeal to form lines and grids that generate in their turn malformed human creatures. It can become the 'bristles' and 'fur' of other forms of supernatural creatures and appear as the tiny multiple 'leaves' of tree- or plant-like forms. It has its origins in and links all the more important elements in the art. Its capacities are

121 (above) The orifices of two oval designs point towards a group of plants surrounded by arrow shapes, and whose forms and white caps derive from oval designs. Mazowe.

123 *One of the largest, most complex and colourful of all the oval designs. Mazowe.*

much greater and more varied than those of any single animal or insect, even one, like the bee, to which some San may have attributed potency and seen as a source of strong supernatural power.

The many paintings of large areas of flecks show how artists conceived of potency pervading their entire surroundings, a force hidden from the naked eye but present everywhere and made visible only through the paintings. Particular forms of potency may have been given particular graphic forms to distinguish them. The association of flecks and trees is particularly strong, strong enough to suggest that flecks represent a particular form of potency that acts primarily on trees, not necessarily trees exclusively but more probably trees as the archetype or epitome of the plant world as opposed to that of man and animals. A parallel can be drawn with the Kung belief that a particular form of potency, *now*, influences the natural world and weather.[26] In this sense, flecks are indeed concerned especially with landscape, not to represent it but to influence it. It is the failure to distinguish between illustration and symbol that has led to the failure to recognise the true significance of the motif. Flecks, far from being a rudimentary method of representing elements in nature and landscape, seem to be a means of delineating a force that permeates nature and landscape.

5

GODS AND SPIRITS

All San seem to have recognised a single supreme deity. He created all things. He gave people knowledge and their first weapons and equipment and is the ultimate source of their potency and indeed all potency, of which he himself has an overpowering and dangerous amount. He looks like a man, is married and has children. He walks the earth, invisible to all but those whose potency is particularly strong and active, engaging in the same activities as men, such as hunting, and having all the qualities, emotions, passions and failings of mankind. He has been guilty of the gravest and most repulsive breaches of morality, including incest and cannibalism. He created and dispenses evil, sickness, misfortune and death. He does not necessarily control human affairs and is believed to be remote and to take only a vague and intermittent interest in them. He is arbitrary and capricious and not much concerned with human morality or in making judgements, ascribing guilt or giving rewards or punishments.

San relationships with their deity are continuous, intimate, easy, relaxed and without reverence. He is loved, despised and treated with levity. Prayer is simple, informal and conversational. It may include questioning, cajolery, complaints, reprimands, scolding and cursing, earthy humour, insults and bargains, pleading and persuasion. Those in trance may come close enough to the gods to engage in struggles with them, at very high risk to themselves.

Beside the supreme god, many San seem to have recognised a second god with his own particular responsibilities. He has even greater failings than the supreme god and is even more hostile, threatening, malevolent and restless. He is usually envisaged as incompetent, ugly, dwarfish, bad tempered and morose and is often characterised as a trickster. Some San groups also gave a special place to the wife of the supreme god; she played a part in creation, giving birth to some animals and holding them in her particular care and affection.

There does not appear to be any direct visual realisation of these beliefs in the paintings of Zimbabwe. Because the gods take entirely human forms and engage in completely human activities, it could be argued that representations of them could well be indistinguishable to us from those of ordinary humans. This seems improbable but at present all one can say is that no apparently human figures are regularly given the emphasis and significance, be it in size, activities, emblems, attributes or contexts, that might suggest that they represent deities. Only the pairs of distended female figures with their complex range of attributes suggest the complex generative, creative and transforming powers of gods. But there is nothing in surviving San ritual or lore to suggest that any believed in a pair of female deities.

The Spirit World

All San studies suggest a belief in peoples' personal survival after death as spirits. The Kung 'believe strongly and vividly in the existence of spirits of the dead ... they fear them, pray to them to invoke their mercy or sympathy, exhort them in anger'. The creator god takes the spirit from a dead person in the form of heart and blood and turns these into a *gauwa*. *Gauwasi* 'have bodies which resemble those they had on earth except for their hair ... eat the same food as humans ... have their own implements, weapons, karosses etc. and keep their own spouses. They descend from the sky on strong, invisible cords and move about on earth ... They are sure to come to [trance] dances and are always there in the shadows and are visible to people in trance'. They are 'associated within peoples' minds primarily with sickness and death,' are conveyors of great evils but not wholly evil.[27]

There are some recurrent images among the paintings that seem to suggest very particular types of creatures engaged in the same sorts of activities as those of humans and with many human attributes but which are emphatically not human. They have long pointed ears and long, sharply pointed muzzles. The limbs of most of them are long thin stick-like lines with no indications of shape or muscle, completely fleshless, reduced to a bony essence, scarcely able to support any weight at all. They are often so thin and elongated, as fragile and long-reaching as a spider's legs, yet they are always carefully jointed in a completely human way. Insect-like, incorporeal, weightless,

124 *Two male figures yet wearing capes, whose long thin limbs, pointed faces and kudu ears constitute a distinct type of image. Bindura.*

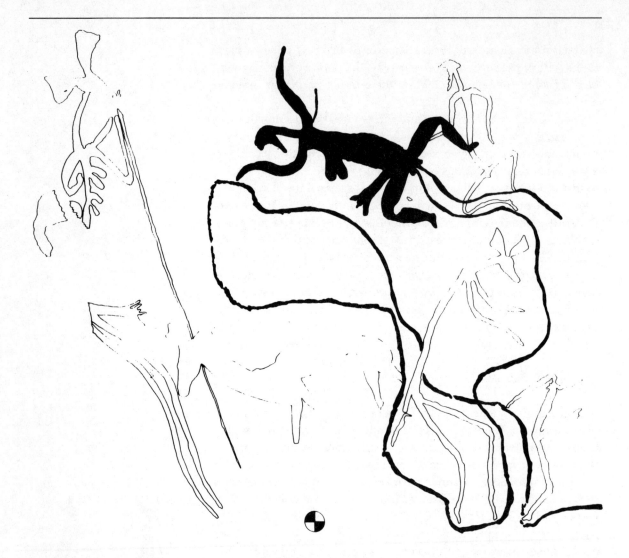

125 *Two similar attenuated figures, one an aproned woman leaning on a stick. Lines come from the enlarged genitalia of another aproned woman though she is not distended. They appear to entangle the other figures. Her partner is beside her in the same 'squatting' posture. Makonde.*

ethereal wraiths, they still sit and walk and gesture in completely, even exaggeratedly human ways that further heighten the ghostly and surreal effects of their proportions. Their gestures emphasise their humanity as their bodies deny it. These figures do not seem to be expressions of human sensations, not even the more extreme sensations of trance. They are also more than transformations, more than partial replacements of human with animal attributes, more than conflation or addition. Something, indeed almost everything, has departed from their bodies, leaving only disembodied action. They convey a sense not of the otherness of human trance, but of the humanity of other beings. They may then represent spirits with only the remote residues of their bodies, almost entirely unworldly and ethereal.

In fig. 125, similar creatures, one at least with a woman's breasts, have ears that are immediately identifiable as those of a kudu and their heads are also those of an antelope. Again they are so long and thin that one fears that their limbs must fracture; one has to support herself with a long stick. Another is encircled by the lines issuing from a woman. In fig. 126 two of these creatures attack each other with clubs; they have large ears, long pointed faces, thin limbs and tails so long that they remind us of the cords that the Kung believe are attached to spirits. In fig. 127 two of these creatures sit on the cusps of an oval design and bleed from their muzzles; again, the way they sit and hold out their arms is particularly lifelike. Very similar pointed ears and muzzle have been given to some of the more elaborate of the distended figures, as in fig. 97, and to a small figure in fig. 178 with more normal proportions, but with lines coming from its abdomen.

In fig. 115 two small examples of these images have been placed among the men who assist in shedding flecks over tree forms. Both

126 *The long 'tails' of these figures 'fighting' in a characteristic fashion may refer to San beliefs that spirits descend from their world to earth on long cords. Mutoko.*

127 *Two figures, seated on the cusps of ovals and bleeding from the points of their muzzles. Mutoko.*

128 The same figures crawl on all fours towards a design like the inverted cap of an oval and gradually stand upright. The figure at the bottom right holds up a similar shape. Bindura.

have long ears, pointed muzzles and alert, lively postures. Both have extraordinary long straight lines ending in a tuft, closely similar to those normally added to some penises. These emerge directly from the genital area, though the figures have no genitals. The men round them all have the same. This establishes that a close relationship, presumably one of potency, deliberately associated all the main actors in this scene. The little figures can then be taken as ethereal onlookers or participants in the main action, witnesses to an act generating a spiritual potency and themselves from a world outside the visible.

In fig. 128 five or six of these figures, some with tails and ears that are bent over at the tips, approach a single simple oval shape. As they get nearer they rise from a low crouch to walk on all fours, then to reach upwards and finally perhaps to stand erect, seeming to gather strength progressively with their increasing proximity to the oval. The group is thus reminiscent of the figures that attach themselves to the potency of the lines that emanate from trancers and distended figures.

One-Legged Figures

One-legged figures are a significant component of the art. Very detailed examples are attached to lines from the distended figures. In fig. 129 there is a group of seventeen of them. Most of these also lack one or both arms. None has any accessories or relationships with other images that would throw light on their exact nature. This group can be contrasted with the two finely painted and detailed kneeling figures below them, beside a smaller and equally fully human recumbent figure. They also contrast with the two large figures striding out with their arms linked on the right, once outlined in white dots. Their large heads contrast with the linear forms of their limbs, so attenuated that they suggest the sense of disembodiment of the other figures we have been studying.

129 *A cluster of one-legged figures bend forward in unison, top left. The two large figures on the right, and the smaller figure imitating them, have disproportionately large heads and attenuated limbs, which contrast with their convincing movements. Wedza.*

130 *Four one-legged figures with leaf shapes attached to them, holding up crescents and hitherto unknown objects formed by two lines; their bags below them have equally unusual forms. Murewa.*

131 *One-legged figures on and above a line that emerges from a distended woman. Their arms are decorated with bangles, their heads twisted unnaturally backwards and white tusks rise from their jaws. Mutoko.*

In fig. 130 four one-legged similar figures are painted in three colours. They face the front to allow full emphasis on their huge, oval, mantis-like eyes and long pointed ears, though losing the shapes of the faces. Each stands on a single leg. Again, each leg has been painted with far too much care and detail for this not to have been an intentional and significant feature of the image.

Semi-Human Figures

Small semi-human figures crouch, crawl along, cling to and float above the lines emitted by distended figures. They are all curiously incomplete. Some have formless bodies and stubby, shortened limbs without joints. Limbs can be absent altogether; some of the more carefully painted, detailed and elaborate of these figures lack a leg or arm or both.

In fig. 157 such figures crawl towards, clamber up and cling to the same sets of lines when they rise from a recumbent figure. In fig. 132 some of the flecks cohere in a line and are bounded by two long lines to make a ladder-like form. The same deliberately roughly sketched little figures hold onto and crawl along this. More flecks seem to cluster over their backs and to one of the lines.

Thus, though it may not often be explicitly realised, distended figures, trancers, ovals and fields of flecks have important relationships in common with semi-human figures. The power they generate transforms human-like beings. It does not create them: in fig. 157 some of the little beings are crawling towards the lines, so must already have been in existence prior to attaching themselves to the

132 *A detail of fig. 117, showing malformed figures on a grid of flecks. Makonde.*

lines. Whether these figures are to be interpreted as humans in some process of alteration or growth, trancers in transformation or creatures of another non-human realm or the spirit world remains to be seen.

The action of their potency on human or semi-human figures links together, in a single conceptual unity, the distended figures, the lines they emit, trancers, ovals and flecks. All are sources of common transforming potency. In analyses, and especially comparative analyses, it is such linkages, such patterns of relationships, that are the most important evidence towards interpretation, the most penetrating explanatory tool of any art historian concerned with prehistoric art.

6

ANIMALS IN SAN BELIEFS AND ART

All San seem to have shared a fundamental belief in a unity of creation. In an ancient mythic time, the supreme god created a single living form, 'the people of the early race'. In this first world the differences between all living creatures were obscure: 'animals were people', they behaved in a fully human way and shared all human virtues and vices, emotion and reason, lusts and ambitions, plots and plans. Later, God named and distinguished the different species, and assigned to each a characteristic pattern of behaviour and determined their roles in the world. This amounted to a second creation. Thus, the distinction between animals and people and between different species of animals is neither absolute or eternal but part of a historical process within time.[28]

133 *Baboons use their tails as seats, an impossible caprice that invests them with human qualities. Mazowe.*

This process was also conceived in another way: animals evolved from humans. Humanity is overlaid or cloaked in a higher animality. The unity of the two is only superficially disrupted by external appearances. Animals retain elements of their human past and nature; they conceive of themselves as human, are interested and involved in human affairs, will interfere in, help and hinder them. Animal behaviour is no different from human behaviour: it is rational, purposive, directed by values and customs and institutions. Animals have language. Some practise sorcery. Their knowledge transcends that of humans in some areas, for instance, in their ability to foretell rain. A consequence of the interpenetration of the worlds of people and animals is that 'animals know all things', 'they know things that we don't', they know what is going to happen: 'an animal is a thing which knows of our death'.[29]

People and animals inhabit a single world in relations of equality, respect, interdependence and co-operation. Animals and people are kin, hence the feelings people retain of closeness, tenderness, indulgence and protectiveness towards animals and why they were seen as so aesthetically captivating and beguiling. Animals and man share a common purpose, a personal and moral relationship. The interconnection between man and nature means that man has no mastery over nature but all his acts can affect it. Man has to allow and assist nature to take its course. The world constitutes a moral order and this order has to be respected.

The San defined and classified their world in several different ways. These are not contradictory or exclusive but rather fulfilled different functions and the San were able to move readily and without confusion from one mode of classification to another. All San groups appear to have recognised a basic division between 'clawed' (or 'pawed') and 'hoofed' creatures. The hoofed creature was benign and beneficent, a creature of herds and communal society, harmless and a provider of meat, at home in daylight. The eland was an exemplar of the hoofed creature, the epitome of goodness in the natural world. The clawed creature – exemplified by the lion – had all the most undesirable human qualities, a solitary and antisocial predator of the night, wandering at a time when everyone else was asleep, liable to attack and kill anyone. It was even more fearsome because of the disturbing similarities between it and people. Like them, it dislikes eating in exposed situations, it disembowels its prey as soon as it is killed, buries the stomach and then carries the carcass away to a convenient place to feed. Lions are believed to have the same powers as particularly powerful and malevolent trancers and to do the same things. This classification was not limited to simply describing purely physical distinctions but was based on fundamental characteristics of

134 *A herd of zebra, some of them very young. Each animal is complete and distinct from the rest. Mazowe.*

behaviour. Crocodiles and snakes were, for instance, classified as pawed creatures and, among the Nharo, the first white colonists were immediately classified as 'pawed creatures'.

Animals provided meat, the most desirable of foods. Animals were classified as 'red', 'black' or, in some classifications, 'white' meat. The most desirable meat was the red meat of large game species such as eland and smaller antelope like the steenbuck and duiker. Black meat was of its nature considered less edible and included the wildebeest and waterbuck, both with tough lean flesh and also, surprisingly, the very palatable and fat meat of the warthog. The fox and jackal were

135 *A lion stands over a small antelope, its neck extended and forelegs bent in death. Bindura.*

also black meat. White meat was inedible and repulsive, particularly when it was of creatures who ate human flesh. It thus included carnivores like the hyena and lion, crocodiles and also snakes, legeuaans and, again surprisingly, hares. The classifications of meat are not only concerned with edibility but with potency. Red meat contains much potency and is appropriate for use in rituals such as a boy's first kill. Black meat has much less potency and is only used in ritual if there is no red meat available. The elephant has all three types of meat in it and hence is considered to have remarkable potency.

Not all creatures were of sufficient interest to merit recognition and identification as distinct species. Some of the smaller antelope and many of the different species of small animals, like the hares and rabbits and smaller birds, were not even named if they were inedible and harmless. They were lumped together in broad generic categories.

Animals in the Paintings

In Zimbabwe it is clear that the paintings are not simply celebrations of animals' beauty or their value as physical sustenance, as sources of food. A strong if not entirely rigid process of selection determined what animals were painted and how they were painted. Paintings of kudu dominate. Tsessebe and, to a lesser extent, sable and zebra are well represented, all of them considered 'red' meat by the San. Many creatures were seldom if ever painted. There are extremely few paintings of eland, waterbuck, reedbuck, impala or wildebeeste. Yet all these animals are equally common large game animals, found in large herds, easily hunted and prime sources of meat (though the meat of wildebeeste and waterbuck are classified as 'black' meat by some San and are certainly leaner and less palatable than that of the others). Small antelope like the oribi and duiker were common subjects but seldom painted with the careful detail that enables species to be identified, just as they were sometimes not distinguished verbally.

Paintings of the dangerous, solitary and fearful 'pawed creatures', with 'black' or the disgusting and forbidden 'white' meat, are much rarer. Depictions of lions, cheetah and jackals can be found, even very occasionally shown in groups or even standing over their dead prey. When they occur, these images are usually so small, careless and

136 *A creature with human legs and stance, but with a feline head, tail and fore-paws. Above, a human figure has been left deliberately incomplete. Mazowe.*

137 *A tiny wildebeeste enclosed in a circle, two invented creatures and an ostrich. Mazowe.*

138 *A waterbuck, identifiable by the distinctive circle on its rump. It has two white lines across each knee. Bindura.*

lacking in detail that the species depicted are generally not identifiable. The striking markings of some of these beasts, like the leopard or cheetah, were also almost universally ignored. Birds and reptiles are as rare and painted with the same disregard for pattern, colouration or emphasis on any distinguishing features that might make their species identifiable. Paintings of fish and crocodiles occur a little more often. Oddly to us, crocodiles are almost always shown from above or below, emphasising their full rounded bellies rather than their fearsome jaws. The rock rabbit or hyrax, ubiquitous animal of the granite hills, shelters and caves and that most closely associated with the paintings in terms of physical proximity and presence, seems never to have been portrayed. Other animals that frequent and seek refuge in the hills, baboons, monkeys, porcupines or klipspringers, were uncommon subjects.

In all the paintings of animals there seems to be a strong emphasis on females. Far more hornless female kudu and tsessebe are to be seen, despite the fact that the horns of male antelope make identification so much easier. Paintings of female elephants outweigh those of males. Paintings of young are as rare as they are with humans, though there is one panel of paintings, fig. 141, that is very largely devoted to the young, small and defenceless of many different species. So clear is this that there seems little doubt that the painters of it recognised a common abstract factor – defencelessness or vulnerability – between all these otherwise different creatures.

Some researchers, particularly P. Vinnicombe, have indeed interpreted the animal imagery as representing in a symbolic way such abstract human qualities, in much the same way as animals like the dog, lion or peacock have been used in some Western art to symbolise qualities like loyalty, bravery or vanity. This panel would seem to lend some support to this approach. However, it is improbable that San perceived any animals in this way in their paintings. Their use of symbolism in Zimbabwe was more detailed and directly derived from more specific aspects of their basic beliefs. A closer analogy would be between their use of animal symbolism – or any other of their symbolic forms – and that of Christian art where animals like the dove, pelican or lamb were incorporated in the iconography as symbols of different aspects of divinity or the divine sacrifice, the central tenet of that religion, as a belief in potencies, was the central belief of San religion.

Even more than the human imagery, animals stand as isolated images in the paintings and do not refer to individual animals or specific activities. They are often shown in graceful movement but they are seldom engaged in anything more specific. There are virtually no scenes of herds, of fear, panic, stampeding, browsing, grazing, drinking, stalking, hunting, killing, or feeding off their prey, fighting, mating, pregnancy, giving birth or suckling. Family groups are far less frequent than is the case with humans. Animals, like humans, are shown without defects, individuality or idiosyncrasy and in an idealised, generalised and archetypal way. It is frequently very difficult to determine the extent to which many juxtapositions, associations or relationships between animal and human images were intended. It is even more difficult to establish the degree and nature of their significance.

Details of the animal imagery often indicate that the artists deliberately sought to distance their subjects from the natural world. Most paintings elongate the bodies of animals just as they do the bodies of people. Many paintings of many different animals are covered with patterns of dots, flecks or networks of lines in white that have no reference to any natural colouration. Considering the poor adhesion of the white pigments it is likely that a great many more paintings were originally adorned in the same ways. Given the significance we have already established for them, these dots and flecks can be taken as references to the animals' potency. Much more common, and again probably originally a great deal commoner, are sets of two or three

139 *A crocodile seen from above or below. Its head is anomalous and its form resembles that of a distended woman; its unpainted belly is reminiscent of an oval. Mazowe.*

140 *A monkey springs. Guruve.*

141 *A panel that appears to have focused on small, young and defenceless animals. It also includes the outlines of an oval composition adorned with whisks, discs and bristles; the large outline of a rhino with her calf behind her; and a line of kneeling figures, top left, all holding their abdomens and with whisks on their shoulders, extended progressively by different artists. Makonde.*

parallel white stripes painted across the necks and knees of many animals, perhaps particularly kudu, tsessebe and buffalo. These again cannot have any reference to anything in nature. They are painted in exactly the same way as necklaces and bangles on human figures, perhaps particularly dancers. That this association was intended is demonstrated in paintings that directly juxtapose animals and humans who are identically decorated with these white lines. The significance of animals decorated with necklaces and bangles may be elucidated by accounts that some San considered their adorn-

142 *An elephant, outlined and adorned with white lines, including double stripes across its legs. Below is a distended figure holding a crescent and surrounded by flecks. Murewa.*

143 A kudu cow superimposed on an oval design. It has white lines across its knees and a line leading from these to the outline of a rectangle. Murewa.

ments of strings of shell beads as a specific indicator of their humanity. Hence these stripes of white paint on animals may be considered as an emblem created and used to denote that animals wearing these shared in the same essential humanity.

All this goes to show that without doubt, in their dealings with animals in the art, artists followed a common agenda in what they portrayed and how they portrayed it and in the references they made through the emblems that they added to such paintings. What this signified is only in part discernible.

The Elephant in Zimbabwe Art

In his early, most closely argued, convincing and important work, Lewis-Williams examined the significance of the eland antelope in the paintings of the Drakensberg.[30] They form by far the most numerous and most elaborately and carefully painted of all the images in that region. He showed the central place they occupied in San myths where the eland was the animal closest to and most loved by God, and in the most important rituals marking people's passage through life: in the rituals surrounding a girl's entry to puberty and a boy's entry to manhood with his first successful eland hunt and in marriage and trancing. He showed how some of its peculiar physical features and behaviour singled it out: the ease with which it could be hunted, the lack of stamina that made it docile and easily driven when it was tired, the great amounts of fat it carried which were believed to be among the most powerful of all sources of potency. He also showed

144 *Two elephants are hunted. One is about to be speared. A man with a spear or staff with a large triangular head looks on and waves a whisk. Makoni.*

how an eland's behaviour as its death approached was seen as strikingly similar to that of a person entering trance – it also bled from the nose, its hair also stood on end, it lowered its head, staggered and fell. The eland thus became a key symbol of potency, its death a metaphor for trance.

Can anything similar to this be recognised in the paintings of Zimbabwe? One cannot, of course, have the same recourse as Lewis-Williams to exegesis. Nothing can now be known of the place of any animals in the myths or rituals of the San of Zimbabwe. Certainly no paintings have been found that suggest the eland played the same role in Zimbabwe that it did in the Drakensberg. Though it was as common in Zimbabwe as anywhere, it was in fact painted so rarely that there seems to have been some principle operating in the art that precluded it from the canon. The animal most frequently painted in Zimbabwe was instead the kudu and especially the kudu cow, but these were seldom painted in any apparent meaningful association

with humans and exhibit no behaviour similar to the eland's in life or imagery.

There is one animal, though it is far from being the one painted most often, that does seem to have had in Zimbabwe the greatly heightened significance of the Drakensberg eland. This is the elephant. It has already been stated that few paintings show anything but the smallest creatures being hunted. The most important exception to this are paintings of elephants being killed. These are few and far between but when they appear they are large, carefully detailed, vivid and animated compositions. Hunters surround the beast, often in great numbers, running towards it and firing arrows at it from every side, fleeing and falling beneath it. Often some of the hunters carry spears and aim and prepare to throw these at the animal, the only instances of this weapon in the art. In fig. 146, a hunter seems to crouch under an elephant and be about to cut the tendon of the hind leg, to hamstring it. As in this instance, both arrows and spears very often have large triangular, crossed and barbed heads. In some cases the elephant is pierced by many arrows and blood, indicated by flecks, flows from the wounds and particularly from the trunk, an indication that it is bleeding internally. Often the animal is disproportionately large in comparison to its hunters.

It is difficult to accept that these scenes record a normal or common activity or even that they could have occurred at all. Elephants would

145 *A wounded elephant bleeds profusely. Agitated hunters surround it, some aiming arrows with large triangular heads. Mazowe.*

146 *Three hunters with spears approach an elephant and a fourth, beneath it, thrusts a spear with a large head at one of its legs. Mazowe.*

147 *An elephant attacked by two hunters. Northern Makonde.*

certainly have been a desirable prey in so far as they would provide large amounts of very palatable meat and fat. But they would also have been extremely difficult if not impossible to kill by the methods shown. Traditionally, elephants could only be killed by constructing concealed pits into which they fell or by using weapons with massive, solid and heavy iron heads – axes and spears – with which to hamstring them or stab them from a safe vantage point. Kalahari San claim that they were impossible to hunt before they had horses and guns. Killing them with arrows was surely near impossible and certainly impossible using arrows with the large, fragile and blunt heads so often shown. These could not have pierced a hide as proverbially tough and thick as an elephant's, let alone penetrated deeply enough into the body to induce trauma sufficient to cause internal haemorrhage.

These paintings then depict extremely improbable, if not impossible, events. If this is combined with the almost complete absence of any record in the art of what must have been the normal hunting of large antelope and similar animals, the significance of these paintings must lie elsewhere. The death of the elephant was perceived as a metaphor for the death of trance. The elephant is the trancer, its blood and particularly that flowing from its trunk parallel the blood – the potent blood, the potency – of the trancer. In both, trance or death is induced and potency activated by arrows of potency. The elephant hunt is the trance dance.

Is there any way to confirm this? Powerful support comes from the similarities in the ways in which paintings of ovals and elephants are

148 *An elephant pin-cushioned with an inordinate number of arrows and bleeding profusely. Goromonzi.*

manipulated in the art. Very large paintings of elephants sometimes in outline and scarcely visible, sometimes now only a faded stain on the rock surface, once dominated many large sets of paintings and even whole caves, which is a general indicator of the subject's importance. Often these were painted over many sets of smaller images, incorporating them, drawing them together into a new conceptual rather than visual unity, becoming the field of force within which the minor images act out their being. Oval designs were used in just the same way. Sometimes ovals and elephants used like this were juxtaposed. Sometimes one is superimposed on the other. In fig. 11, a large elephant has been superimposed on an oval pattern which has expanded and developed as more and more ovals were fitted round the

149 *An elephant whose serrated back derives from the pattern formed by a line of capped cores in an oval design. It has only two legs and bleeds from arrow wounds. Murewa.*

150 (above) and fig. 151 (right). Three further elephant-like creatures with cusped or serrated backs, all from the same cave. Between the lower pair is a creature with human features but whose arms extend to suggest wings. Murewa.

XXVI (opposite) An elephant decorated with white stripes. The male figures have tufts on their buttocks. The emblem attached to their penises is found most often in situations where potency is likely to be most active. Mutoko.

edges of the composition. The elephant takes the place of the ovals, is their equivalent. Conclusive confirmation that the two images share similar qualities can be found where elephant and ovals are conflated. Something of this is suggested by small paintings of trunked creatures with deeply serrated backs, one at least with flecks flowing from its body and trunk. But it is finally confirmed in a large painting of which almost all that now remain are the dark outlines of the body and legs and the pale stain of the body colour, in which the back is entirely formed by a careful and unmistakable line of cusps identical in form to the tops of a characteristic line of ovals. It establishes the conceptual identity of elephants and ovals at least at some level.

Other Hunted Creatures

Can this be carried further? Two other species of animals – rhino and buffalo – were treated like the elephant. Very large images of them, often in outline, were painted, juxtaposed with, incorporating or providing the field for a large number of smaller images. And there are also paintings of these two species being hunted with arrows and spears with the same heads as those used against elephants, wounded and bleeding like the elephant. The three are the largest, most unpredictable, ill-tempered and dangerous of animals, the most difficult to hunt, yet the sources of large amounts of very desirable meat. They were not the animals usually hunted. One further image occurs often enough to form a consistent sub-theme to these: that of zebra bleeding internally with blood coming as lines from the nostrils and mouth and forming a pool below the hanging head. This is a far more common and likely prey than the large beasts, but it is only once

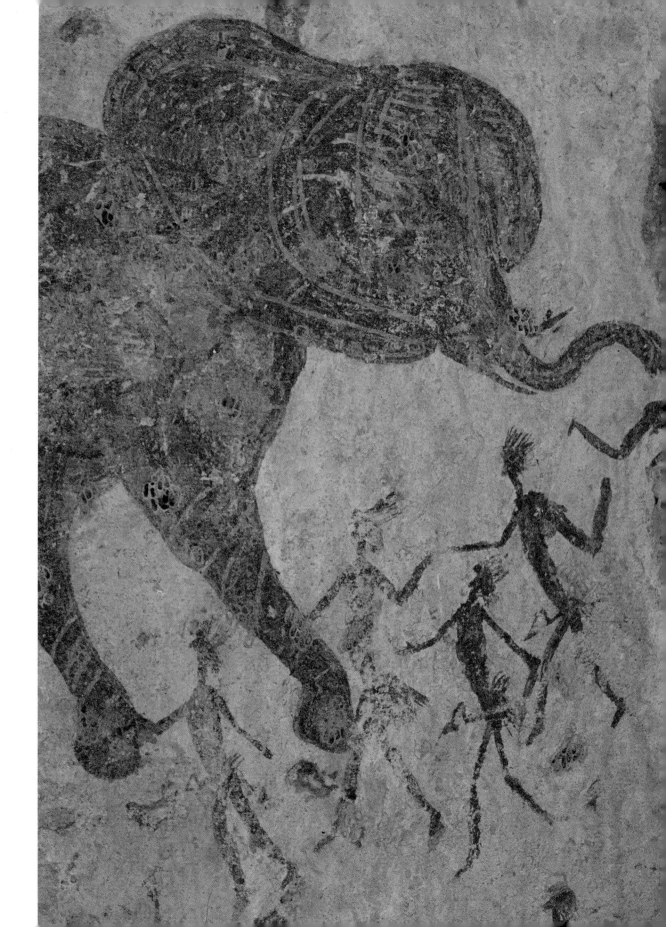

XXVII (above) A general view of the elephant shown in plate XXVI. Few of the many men around it are armed; the tufts they wear are suggestive of a dance. The potency represented by the animal is being released and absorbed through dancing rather than through the usual metaphor of a hunt. Mutoko.

XXVIII (below) Friezes of baboons and people encamped are dominated by the two most significant themes in the art: the large elephant and the two oval designs. The larger has been badly damaged by bullets fired at it by servicemen training in the area during World War II. Guruve.

XXIX (above) An elephant superimposed over human figures, many of them resting in family groups, archetypes of the domestic virtues. Again the ovals of potency are a prominent feature, bottom right. Marondera.

XXX (below) Hunters surround the outline of a large animal, probably a rhinoceros. In the centre, as a distinct scene, parents embrace on their blankets, surrounded by their possessions. Details from this panel are shown in figs 48, 57 and 82. Makonde.

XXXI *One of the best-preserved and most elaborate painted panels in Zimbabwe. Details are shown in the next four plates. Makoni.*

XXXII *and* **XXXIII** *The great recumbent figure of an archetypal trancer. The positions of his arms and legs demonstrate that he is fully conscious and in control of his actions. His body is covered in the white dots of latent potency, as is the oval of potency that is attached to the back of his abdomen. A tendril emerges from his penis, passes behind his legs and ends in a charactersitic tuft. His face is painted with the markings of a sable antelope. Comparative analysis suggests that the lines rising from his head are derived from elephant tusks and are not horns. In the same way, the lines falling from his head may have suggested a lion's mane. Makoni.*

XXXIV *(above) Baskets, skins and gourds, all embellished with the white dots of potency, place the figures below them in a domestic situation, the one in which dancing normally occurs. The curved lines suggest temporary windbreaks or shelters. Makoni.*

XXXV *(opposite) Lines of dark figures painted with the white chests, bellies and undersides of their limbs, facial stripes and eye surrounds that identify them with sable antelope. Dots of potency enhance their genitals. They represent participants in a Sable Dance, which reached its climax in the trancing of the great figure at the top. Even the dog-like creature, bottom centre, has the same markings and emblems of tusks and mane, making him a transformation of the dancers themselves. Similar white details probably once enhanced most paintings in Zimbabwe. Makoni.*

xxxvi *An oval design, surrounded by the dark flecks of active potency, has been placed over seated and crouched figures and a large kudu bull. Matobo.*

shown being hunted. And there are no large paintings of it used as a unifying element for other paintings.

As ovals and elephants were, to some extent at least, interchangeable, the conceptual equivalence of buffalo and elephant is also established visually. In fig. 184 the large outline of a buffalo has been painted over that of an earlier elephant. The backs of the two coincide closely.

152 *A hunter prepares to launch a spear towards a buffalo, its head lowered in its weakness. Flecks give significance to the scene. Marondera.*

153 *Hunters and a buffalo. The form of arrow characteristic of such scenes is held by the hunter on the right. Goromonzi.*

154 *A zebra with its head lowered in a symptom of death, bleeds from its muzzle. Mutoko.*

155 *A man lies pierced with several arrows. Mutoko.*

The paintings of the Drakensberg include several large and very detailed scenes of battles between groups of armed hunters and men with weapons developed in recent times by other races, some of them white commandos and soldiers. There is nothing like this in Zimbabwe. Few paintings show fighting between groups of people. But there are paintings of individual men, recumbent in the characteristic posture of the trancer, who are pierced by an inordinate number of arrows. Some of their assailants, often much smaller than them, aim further arrows at them, some with the large heads of arrows of potency. These scenes offer further evidence from a new quarter for the interpretation of scenes of hunting and death – of both men and the three archetypal large beasts – as metaphors for the death of trance.

Other Conflations of Animals and Ovals

The conflation of ovals and animals went little further than the creatures based on the elephant, but fig. 156 shows one variation. The composite conceptualised creature has cusps along its back, the two legs of a bird, the trunk of an elephant and the ears of an antelope, perhaps a sable, or possibly even of a zebra.

The other important conflation of this sort was based most closely on a snake. It has the long thin undulating body of a snake but the head of the creatures I have assigned to the spirit world, with long pointed muzzle and antelope's ears, usually those of a kudu. The relationship of these snake-like creatures to a potency generated by one trancer and most distended figures is apparent in fig. 157, where the multiple lines characteristic of the emanations from a distended figure here rise from a trancer and change into one of these snake creatures. There are examples where the backs of these creatures once more form what were originally called 'hills', but can now be seen clearly to be the cusps or caps of ovals. Along them can crawl the

156 *A conceptual two-legged creature with trunk-like nose, antelope ears, two legs and a cusped back. Lines suggesting bleeding come from its chest. Marondera.*

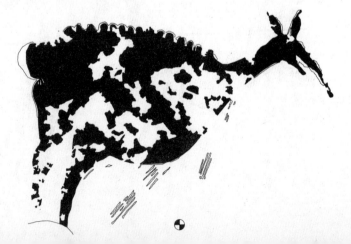

same partly formed or malformed semi-human creations that adhere to the lines coming from distended figures and the trancer of fig. 157, to ladder-like aggregations of flecks and to the cusps of ovals. Here then is another image, one derived from and based most firmly in the animal realm, that was believed and seen to have the same powers.

There are two sets of images that may also use animals as metaphors for different aspects or degrees of trance. Many animals are painted 'upside down'. Sometimes in a line of animals of a single species, one is shown in this way. Comparison with its neighbours shows that it is not, as is popularly said, 'dead'. Its stance and carriage belie this. Its legs and tail are tense, rigid and alive. It is similar to its neighbours in all its details except that it is reversed. In contrast there are other paintings of animals that are indeed dead; they too are 'upside down' but now their bodies are relaxed, their legs limp and bent, their necks stretched and twisted, their heads laid back. These two types of images recur with some frequency and the distinction between them is clear and was clearly intentional and significant. Animals reversed but fully alive are reminiscent of the way the consciousness of the recumbent trancer was established visually by the positioning of his legs, carefully bent and generally with the foot of one leg poised resting on the knee of the other and with his hands often supporting his head. This careful arrangement, signifying the consciousness of a person unable to stand, could not of course be reproduced in animals. Reversed animals may substitute for it. They certainly convey a similar message: they too are 'recumbent' and 'helpless' but still have sufficient control of their limbs to indicate that they are conscious and 'alive'.

There is some reason to suppose that some of the dead animals also correspond to humans in trance. Below the large group of people participating in different aspects of dancing in fig. 73 are groups of small antelope, almost a frieze, the only other paintings on this rock face, and not disturbed or confused by images of hunters or any other animals. This suggests, with less ambiguity than most juxtapositions, that an association between the people and animals was intended. One of the antelope has its head, neck and legs limp, bent and twisted in death, just as there is one person in the main painting who is recumbent among the dance chorus and who has been identified earlier as a trancer. The striking visual correspondences between the two suggests with some strength that the dead animal alludes to the

157 *Lines rising from a recumbent figure transform into a creature with a snake's body and antelope's head. Marondera.*

158 *At the top of this panel are the exfoliated remains of a lion standing over a limp and dead antelope. One of the group of small antelope at the bottom is upside down but nothing else suggests death: its form is otherwise identical to that of its companions. Mazowe.*

'death of trance'. If this is correct, it makes all the antelope in some sense participants in the human trance dance.

In South Africa, a great deal of interest has always been focused on paintings in the Drakensberg of what have unfortunately been named 'therianthropes'. These conflate human and eland elements and have now been shown to be concerned with the potency of the eland, the indigenous animal that the local San believed to be the greatest source of potency, symbolising its many different aspects in their paintings.

There is extremely little in the Zimbabwe paintings that could be called 'therianthropic'. The figures here assigned to the San spirit world, with their pointed animal muzzles and large antelope ears, could be so called but their dominant characteristic is the fragility of their limbs and these remain emphatically human. The best examples in Zimbabwe of conflation of different types of image are those that combine elements of particular animals with key features of the oval designs.

Given their basic unity, boundaries between man and animal are fluid and permeable. Trancers can turn into animals, and animals can transform themselves into humans. There can be no certainty whether any creature you meet is what it appears to be, that it is indeed an animal and not a person. Even God often decided to take an animal form and wander through his creation. Paintings of human figures which have become winged and feathered composite creatures remind one how important creatures with the appearance of birds were for the Xam San at least. There are numerous reports by some of them of what seemed to be birds acting as messengers of the future, as omens and as a favoured form for trancers to take when they travelled in spirit, far and fast as only a bird in flight is able, to visit distant places, and carry news back and forth.

What we cannot yet tell is whether the paintings described here depict trancers in the process of transformation or wholly transformed and inhabiting a bird's body or whether they represent pure spirits, part of the spirit world. Perhaps there are examples of both. Perhaps those associated with recumbent and contorted postures represent trancers. Perhaps the emblem of the tufted line like the tusk indicates that the transformation of a trancer has taken place. Perhaps those with only one leg are in contrast spirits of the dead.

159 *Two of the rare examples of creatures that combine human and antelope characteristics. Matobo.*

160 *The top figure, with lower limbs and body paint in white, has the head of an antelope protruding from its buttocks. A similar figure occurs in fig. 74. This may be a reference to generation. Matobo.*

The relationship of the elephant with potency was established visually still more firmly through the creation of conceptual creatures that conflate the elephant and oval design: creatures with all the features of an elephant but with the length of their backs cusped or serrated with semicircular forms derived from the top caps or cusps of a line of ovals. We have also seen how the elephant and buffalo were the sources, channels or symbols of a potency that acted to generate or transform people or spirits. In the next chapter we shall see how the elephant, through making its tusks a metonym for its transforming power, provided a widespread emblem that was attached to otherwise human and animal images to signify their transformation.

7

EMBLEMS

The human archetypes which we have discussed were qualified very frequently by attaching a range of attributes to them. These seem so simple and specific that they can be considered 'emblems'. We are far from understanding what many of these signify with any precision; the vocabulary is large and their contexts various but at least some patterns of associations are becoming discernible. We have already seen many emblems in use in the paintings. Bows, arrows and narrow shoulder bags signify man in his archetypal role as a hunter. Digging sticks, large collecting bags and aprons signify women as gatherers. All of these are clearly actual objects, the 'tools of the trade' of the archetypes. There is no problem in their identification or in recognising why and how they were chosen as key attributes or emblems to define visually, archetypal male and female roles. Some dancers are similarly identifiable by the tufts and tails that male dancers often wear.

Less readily comprehensible are the shapes or lines of various sorts that many human figures have on their heads: cones, single tufted shapes as in fig. 163, lines of tufts as in fig. 162, lines rising from across the crown, similar lines parted in the middle, lines down the back of the head and lines falling over and covering the face. Almost all are found only on men. Few have commented on them, except to conclude that lines standing up from the head represent a San practice in which hunters stuck arrows in a band tied round their heads so that they were instantly ready for use. Such interpretations cannot be correct. Such lines are found on many figures that are not equipped for hunting. When they are painted on hunters, they are quite different in size and shape to the arrows they have in their bags or carry in their hands.

161 *A male figure with the emblem of a line painted across his genital organ. Goromonzi.*

162 *A figure with tufts on his head, a 'mane' of lines falling from the back of his head, a disc on his shoulder and a tufted line coming from his penis. Harare.*

Men often have one, or occasionally two, short, straight lines painted across their penises. A single tendril-like line, ending in a tufted shape not unlike our conventional image of a tulip, can be attached to one end of the bar or emerge directly from the tip of the penis. Such lines can be shortened, greatly thickened and given a bifurcated or swallow-tailed end as in fig. 28. The thickened form is often broken or sharply angled in the middle. All seem to be variations on a single idea. They cannot, as has often been claimed, represent some form of adornment. Though it is not conclusive, it is important to recognise that there are no records of any San adorning their sexual organs nor of them having any accoutrements that resemble these shapes. Nor can they represent, as has also been frequently suggested, some form of cultural prohibition against, for instance, urination or sexual activity in prescribed circumstances. The best evidence against all such interpretations is that the same forms can emerge directly from a man's navel, as in figs 163 and 164, and in all the figures in fig. 115 and the transforming figures in fig. 83. The same thin lines ending in a small tuft or tulip shape also fall straight downwards from the armpits of some figures, as in the large figures at the bottom of fig. 112, suggesting the particular form of sweat that we have already seen some San equate with potency, a potency that is particularly powerful in healing. Flecks have also been seen to flow from the same source. These signs – the bar and the variations on the tufted line – occur with great frequency, but there does seem to be a tendency for them to be most common in situations where potency is most active. They are uncommon in paintings of men in family groups. Many straightforward paintings of hunters lack them. In general terms it seems that, in ascending order of frequency they are likely to occur in paintings of dancers, of recumbent trancers, of hunters killing dangerous animals, of transforming figures and of men juxtaposed with flecks. The sum of the placements

163 *A figure with a barred line coming directly from his abdomen or navel and a tuft on his head. Goromonzi.*

164 *A recumbent figure holds the tufted line coming from his navel. Marondera.*

and associations of these signs suggests that they were concerned to render visible some supernatural or metaphysical quality inherent inside men's bodies, abdomens or sexual organs that was connected with their spiritual energy or potency. Such signs are probably the most frequent indicators of this concept and indicate how widespread were references to it in the paintings.

Whisks, Leaves and Discs

Hunters almost all have fly whisks protruding from their small, narrow hunting bags along with their arrows; they almost never hold them in their hands. In contrast, lines of men almost entirely without their weapons often hold them or wave them, as in fig. 75. Others in such lines may have them tied to their shoulders, as in the line of kneeling figures holding their abdomens at the top left of fig. 141. The same device occurs on the solitary man standing just below them. In this panel, the outlines of large oval shapes also have small whisks attached to them.

A simple shape – elongated, pointed at both ends and widest in the middle – which I have called a 'leaf shape' or 'leaf' occurs in much the same circumstances as whisks. It too is shown tied to men's shoulders or to their upper arms. Sometimes even the ends of the strings that attach it are visible, hanging down under the arms. Very rarely a hunter holds one in his hands, as do single figures in figs 12 and 49. A less common but regular variation on this emblem are pairs of leaf shapes joined at the base and attached only to the chests or abdomens of men. They seem to occur particularly on recumbent figures. Six of the eleven swaying, falling, crawling and recumbent figures in fig. 165 have them, as does the much larger striding figure with them,

165 *Most of these figures, by different artists, have pairs of leaf-shapes attached to their abdomens. Mutoko.*

probably the primary image of the group. The largest recumbent figure in this group lies in the most characteristic posture of trance and has a tufted tendril attached to his penis. Five of the seven figures in fig. 166 have the same twin leaves on the front or backs of their chests. Most of them have their legs bent and splayed in the posture most closely associated with distended figures. Two again have bars with tufted appendages across their penises.

A third emblem, again a very simple one, occurs in similar circumstances to whisks and leaves. It is a circle on the end of a short straight stem, a 'disc shape', like those that form parts of the penises and arms of some of the hunters we considered earlier, though now it is a distinct object rather than an integral part of the anatomy. These too are attached to the shoulder or upper arm but are seldom held in the hand. Unlike the whisks or leaves however, they may also hang down from the arms, when they usually have small pointed tips so that they look like 'droplets', as in some figures in fig. 75 and the isolated figure in fig. 141, where they hang from the elbow. In this panel discs, like whisks, are also attached to the outlines of ovals.

Three groups of paintings on two faces of a rather sparsely painted rock illustrate wider ramifications of the disc and how the same form could be used in different scenes and different contexts. As more paintings were added to the panel, it provided a unifying element or commentary on apparently disparate subjects. In fig. 167 two hunters

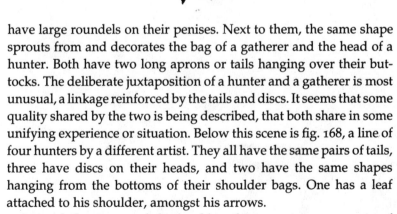

166 *Another group of men with pairs of leaf-shapes coming from their chests. Two have tufts on the ends of the lines attached to the tips of the bars across their penises. Murewa.*

have large roundels on their penises. Next to them, the same shape sprouts from and decorates the bag of a gatherer and the head of a hunter. Both have two long aprons or tails hanging over their buttocks. The deliberate juxtaposition of a hunter and a gatherer is most unusual, a linkage reinforced by the tails and discs. It seems that some quality shared by the two is being described, that both share in some unifying experience or situation. Below this scene is fig. 168, a line of four hunters by a different artist. They all have the same pairs of tails, three have discs on their heads, and two have the same shapes hanging from the bottoms of their shoulder bags. One has a leaf attached to his shoulder, amongst his arrows.

Around the corner of the boulder, there are two more sets of paintings, fig. 169, that may have been intended to amplify and elucidate part of the meaning of the emblem. A line of five women, sketched by yet another artist, all wear aprons and have additions to their heads in the shape of bifurcated tufts. They raise their hands and

167 *Male and female figures with discs on their heads, bags and genitalia. Murewa.*

168 *Hunters with disc shapes on their heads and bags, and pairs of tails hanging over their buttocks. Murewa.*

169 *Aproned and clapping figures with tufts across their heads, below disc-shaped plant forms. Murewa.*

spread their fingers, apparently clapping, an action most frequently used by the women forming the chorus for a dance. They do not have discs attached to their bodies – no woman ever does – but above them is an unusual group of carefully painted if unidentifiable plant forms: tubers, fruits or pods. Each has a short straight stem and their shape is a strong echo of the disc shape, which suggests that they may be its counterpart in the natural world.

In this series of paintings, the same emblem is attached to the genitals, heads and bags of hunters, gatherers and dancers. Taking all these images together and placing them in the context of potency, it seems reasonable to suggest that they are all concerned with a specific form of potency inherent in, associated with or named after a particular 'disc-shaped' plant which, harnessed in dancing, affects and unites both men and women, adheres to and alters their heads, sexual organs and equipment or, putting it figuratively, fills and enriches their bags and their persons, physically as food, mentally and sexually.

Combs

There is a more detailed and complex emblem that is also used in much the same ways as those that have just been analysed. It has a short straight stem or handle which widens into a roughly triangular body. Along both sides of this, short straight lines or 'teeth' project, hence the label 'comb' that has been chosen to describe it. Again it is not possible to identify precisely what these emblems represent; they may be plants or musical instruments like rattles. Again they are tied to people's shoulders or held in their hands. Unlike the whisk, disc or leaf, they never occur singly: people who have them, have one in each hand or one on each shoulder.

Very occasionally, otherwise very ordinary little figures may hold large and detailed combs, as in fig. 170; so can figures so attenuated that they recall spirit figures, as in fig. 171. Most often they are attached to or held by distended figures, as in figs 93, 95, 97 and 99. This association is much stronger than is the case with any other emblem. No hunters or trancers have them; no dancers hold combs; nor does anyone among those groups of men holding such wide arrays of objects and who may also be participating in a particular form of dance.

The distended figures, the strongest and clearest images illustrating the generation of potency, almost always hold combs or leaves. Otherwise they may hold a single, long, curved crescent, another unidentified emblematic object and one that is exclusive to distended

170 A man holds a 'comb' in each hand. Guruve.

171 *Two extremely elongated and attenuated figures hold combs. Guruve.*

figures. Combs and leaves are otherwise only held by men. Whisks and discs are an even more exclusively masculine prerogative: the only distended figure with whisks is a man, fig. 92, and no distended figure has discs. Distended figures are overwhelmingly but not exclusively female yet they bear more emblems than any other figures and these are emblems that are otherwise exclusively male prerogatives: this even includes the lines falling from the backs of their heads, which are otherwise almost only found on men. This suggests that emblems in part were used to construct gender. Sexually these figures are clearly women yet their emblems reconstruct them as men. Indirectly, this harks back once more to San concepts of potency and suggests again that these emblems denote aspects of potency. Though everyone in San society had inherent potency and the potential to activate it, such activation and from it the ability to trance, cure, transform and travel in spirit were predominantly male activities: for instance, three out of four trancers among the Kung San is a man. So these very highly potent women appear through their attributes or emblems to be in some sense redesignated as men.

172 *A line of men, some holding whisks and others arrows of potency and all with pairs of tails hanging from their waists, walk away from their camp, designated by their weaponry and their wives' bags suspended from withies. Bindura.*

Arrows of Potency

In fig. 172 a line of men is striding out and clearly sharing a common purpose. This is not a hunting party: no one carries hunting bags, bows or conventional arrows. This is made very clear by the careful painting of the camp site behind them, which they are leaving, where their bows are carefully stacked beside large bags slung from bent withies (a warthog's head is also impaled on one of the withies). Most have large whisks in both hands and almost all wear a pair of tails hanging over their buttocks and have tufts rising up behind their waists. Whisks held in the hand, tufts and tails denote dancing. The extreme attenuation of the figures and lack of form of their bodies may indicate that they belong to a spirit rather than human realm. These features are deliberately contrasted with a single, normally proportioned and fully armed hunter at the camp site and an aproned woman who claps her hands in front of him. Three carry distinctive arrows with very large spiked and barbed heads formed by crossed lines or lines in the form of a large triangle with its apex attached to the shaft and its broad base pointing forward. We have seen such arrows before: some in the hands of otherwise apparently ordinary hunters, more often held by dancing men and very frequently used by the hunters of elephants and the other dangerous animals; the same heads were also used to arm such hunters' spears. These heads seem so totally impractical as to appear perverse. They are too large

173 *A hunter holds arrows that have large bifurcated spiked and barbed heads. He has roundels on his upper arms and penis and a leaf shape attached to one roundel. Guruve.*

and therefore too heavy to be aerodynamically efficient, to attain any velocity, to travel any distance or be able to pierce the skin of any animal: they have none of the qualities needed in an efficient projectile weapon. They could conceivably have been made of lengths of bone or wood bound together, but this seems highly improbable. Certainly they do not represent stone arrowheads, the only material known to have been used for cutting edges at the time of the paintings. If they existed in the forms shown they look most likely to have been forged in metal yet there is no other evidence of metal in the paintings.

Many San believe or believed that during the course of a trance dance, experienced trancers shoot small, invisible 'arrows of potency' into the abdomens of novice trancers seeking to learn how to activate their potency and enter trance fully. The novices feel the stings of these arrows and their potency would then begin to 'boil' and 'rise through their bodies'. San also believed that malevolent trancers and spirits shot 'arrows of evil' into people to cause sickness. The contexts of those carrying arrows with these characteristic unwieldy heads strongly suggest that they indeed represent arrows of potency. This is particularly apparent in the many paintings of elephants, themselves the dominant metaphor for the potent trancer, their blood a metaphor and more than a metaphor for potency and their killing a metaphor for the death of trance. So it is reasonable to interpret the arrows that so often wound and kill them as the arrows that induce potency. Once this is recognised, it is clear that this emblem was widely used to introduce references to potency in many different situations. The arrow with the completely unrealistic head in a stereotyped form becomes the arrow of potency and its appearance in paint becomes a widespread, striking, immediately legible means of denoting potency.

Tusks

Another recurrent, if less frequent, feature of the imagery are figures which have long lines, thickened at the base and pointed at the tip, curving out and up from people's faces or in pairs attached to their lower jaws and exposed by their gaping mouths. The fearsome figures in fig. 90 all have them; the one-legged figures in fig. 129, attached to lines from a distended woman, have them; the bleeding curer and his patient in fig. 80 both have them; some distended figures, as in fig. 95, may have them. The three delicate little figures in fig. 174 also have them. They are grotesque in other ways as well: their thin and fragile legs contrast with their thick, heavy and shape-

less arms. Triple lines spout from their armpits, chests and elbows and suggest sweat or blood. With two of them, these lines also fall from large, carefully painted circles or receptacles that they hold – objects shown in no other paintings. Three are armed with tiny bows and arrows; two have long-stemmed whisks on one shoulder; all have lines or tufts across their heads.

174 *Small figures with gaping mouths that reveal their 'tusks'. Delicate triple lines fall from different parts of their bodies and the objects they hold. Mazowe.*

175 *Tusked creatures with both human and animal elements. Wedza.*

The one common context for all such images seems to be that all are in a process of change. They are recovering from sickness; their bodies are incomplete, malformed, swollen or even covered in fur, tailed and horned and changing into lions. This emblem may therefore specifically signify or connote transformation. The references of the emblem itself seem to be to elephants, for its shape most closely resembles an elephant's tusk rather than any animal's fangs. And, of course, it has now been well established how powerful the elephant was as a source and symbol of potency.

If this emblem does connote transformation, one could predict that it would be found on creatures that are almost entirely animal-like: trancers who have completed their transformation and almost fully adopted the bodies of animals. Such images can be found. In fig. 175 three creatures have two long curved lines coming from their jaws that resemble tusks particularly closely. They walk on all fours and are more like baboons than anything else though their tails are not long enough and do not have the characteristic sharp curve of a baboon's; their ears are pointed, unlike a baboon's; their fore-paws seem clawed, though this could represent a baboon's fingers; and their hind legs are almost completely human. These images do however suggest the interpenetration of human and animal realms and forms that is so basic to San perceptions and belief, is denoted by tusks and assisted by the potency they signify.

Interpreting Emblems

Even if we cannot yet identify the actual objects that are the basis of many emblems, it is still apparent that they had connotations beyond their specific identity. It is also very clear that the ways that they were used in the paintings followed recognised rules. There were rules about what objects were selected as emblems, how they were represented, who they were attached to and in what situations this was permitted, even if these rules were not entirely rigidly applied. This then is one area of the art in which it is possible that detailed statistical analyses of a wide range of these images – and of images that do not have emblems – may reveal more precisely the contexts in which various emblems were used and hence give more specific indications of their significance.

It is already clear that many emblems were not mutually exclusive: a man may have a whole array of different emblems attached to different parts of his body. Parents may have different emblems or the same emblems attached to them, while children never have any at all. This demonstrates that emblems are not totemic, for in a totemic

system parents do not normally share the same totem and children take the totem of one of their parents. Emblems cannot be badges of different clans, castes, associations or age-grades, because membership of any one of these generally excludes membership of any other. Emblems are not exclusively associated with and hence do not define particular activities; indeed some emblems, notably the leaf, can occur in a wide range of different circumstances – in hunting, dancing, trancing and domestic scenes. They define qualities that cut across the limited range of social roles with which the art is primarily concerned but, with few exceptions, are not shared by both sexes. Most emblems are only painted on men. The additions to the penis obviously have no female equivalent, but discs, whisks and the pairs of leaves on the torso are equally exclusive. The mane is not only almost exclusively male but strongly correlated with hunters. Tusks are similarly almost all on men and seem particularly related to transformed beings; the only exceptions are the manes and possibly tusks on female figures with distended abdomens. Triangles and tufts on the head are the emblems most commonly placed on women but they are found at least as frequently on men. There are no exclusively female emblems.

Given that the imagery was so concerned with generalisation, it seems a contradiction that so many emblems were used to qualify images. An explanation can be suggested. The primary concern of the art was to present people as social beings. The essence of a person's social and economic being was relatively easy to describe visually, through tools, weapons, equipment, clothing and postures, all of which had an immediate and obvious correspondence with palpable reality. However, given San beliefs that the natural and supernatural spheres were indivisible and that each permeated the other, and their beliefs in the pervasive presence of personal potency, and given the concern in the paintings with expressing the essential elements of humanity, it might be expected that the art would pay a great deal of attention to establishing and defining the metaphysical capabilities and roles of people as well as their social and economic responsibilities, more so because their spiritual capacities were of the essence of people as social beings. Many San conceived of themselves as more individual in their supernatural capacities than in their social roles. The Xam recognised 'four overlapping categories' of trancers, those concerned with rain, game, illness and those without such specific capacities. In Kung hunting-gathering groups, all men hunted and all women gathered but only about a third of the men and a tenth of the women developed the will and energy to activate and use their supernatural potential and trance. There was also a great variety of different sorts of potency, activated by different dances and songs, in different circumstances and associated in an elusive way with different animals and plants. There were also different degrees of potency, controlled and uncontrolled, dormant, active and transforming. There was strong and weak potency, good and bad, social and antisocial, malevolent, harmful, deathly, creative or healing. Trancers were in a sense the only specialists in San society.

Supernatural qualities were, of their nature, mysterious, ill-defined and invisible: concepts embedded in belief rather than percepts derived from reality. They were correspondingly more difficult to depict. The structure of the art already suggests that aspects of potency will not be represented by simple illustrations of what happens or what particular people did in particular circumstances. It will rarely illustrate in detail activities associated with potency such as curing, influencing game, rain-making or travelling as spirits. Rather, we are likely to find that figures will be given a prescribed and limited range of attributes that signify particular supernatural qualities. The relationship between visual image and concepts of spiritual power could only be largely indirect and conventional. These are difficult for someone outside the culture to recognise, understand or interpret. In so far as emblems refer to or symbolise metaphysical qualities, their significance can only be teased out from the patterns of their associations and contexts.

If many paintings were concerned with depicting potency, it is probable that there is, for us, a difficult, imperfectly understood

'sub-text' to all the paintings that is concerned with describing various aspects of it. It was perhaps a dominant theme of the paintings and one that was readily comprehensible to the original audience but is not to us. What seem to us to be realistic representations of ordinary people in ordinary situations may on one level be just that but they were painted by San artists within a San system of beliefs for a San audience. They are therefore likely to use San modes of description to carry information about San metaphysics.

8

RELATIONSHIPS BETWEEN PAINTINGS

The rock paintings of Zimbabwe are visual realisations of the perceptions of the artists' societies of their world in its natural, supernatural, social and ideological dimensions. The paintings are constructs of the artists' understanding of people's roles in their societies, of the relationships between the living and the dead, between man and animal, between man and the spirits of the dead and man and the gods. Above all, they image the supernatural energies inherent in almost all living things, the forces that gave meaning and significance to the world, to life and to all human and animal activity, the forces that made them fully what they were, that enabled them to transcend what they appeared to be. The art is the exploration of a culturally constructed world, one specific to the culture of the artists.

It is an imagery of ideas, of things believed in rather than of things seen. The emblems attached to people, on their heads, emerging from many different parts of their bodies, defacing their penises, added further content to the imagery. Actual objects – whisks, discs, combs, leaves, arrows with large heads – also acquired additional conceptual content which promoted them to emblems. This is apparent even though we are not yet able to say exactly what this added content was or even to identify the majority of these objects.

The art is concerned with specific ideas, beliefs and perceptions. It is primarily a rational expression of these ideas, conditioned by them and designed to explore, celebrate and instil them. In its essence it is the expression of a single coherent system of thought, one generated by a society as a whole. It is only in minor ways the creation of individuals. Individual artists might delight in and focus most of their attention on and refine particular aspects of the system.

By definition, the paintings are visual. All carry references to the visible world as seen through human artists' eyes. But the subjects are also all vehicles developed to carry an ideological and metaphysical content. The human figures, for instance, are clearly idealised, generalised, stylised and distilled to an ideological essence. It may look less obvious to some but the same is just as true of paintings of animals and plants.

Like all visual art, the art is autonomous. Like all visual art, it operates in very different ways from verbal or oral communication. Specifically, this particular art is not concerned with time sequences, with narrative, be it as a record of significant social, historical or ritual occurrences, or remembrances of personal incidents significant only to the individual artist. It is only the most indirect reflection of fable, myth or legend. Even less is it an illustration of stories invented round the camp fire. The paintings do not form a code; they do not carry verbal messages. It is absurd to propose that images can be transposed or reduced to some visual equivalent of nouns, verbs, sentences and paragraphs, as has recently been attempted.

A specific system of visual representation was developed, dependent on outline to the almost complete exclusion of all else, on a system of continually changing or multiple viewpoints, each focused on defining the basic elements of every subject. Each individual image is an aggregation of these elements. The system demoted colour, texture, surface, light, atmosphere and actual surrounding or context. The aim was quick definition of a very limited range of points, easy legibility and immediate recognition, not accurate reproduction.

Compared with the Drakensberg paintings, or rather with the interpretations now current of those paintings, comparatively little in the human imagery in Zimbabwe is directly illustrative of aspects of trancing. There are some scenes that illustrate dancing clearly and directly but they are comparatively few. Even fewer, no more than two known examples, represent practices known to be associated with San curing. A small and specific set of characteristic postures seems to have been developed to signify trancers; they lie recumbent, inert but fully conscious, one foot on the other knee, holding their heads or chests in one or both hands.

Some distortions of the human figures may describe experiences of trance. The roundels on upper arms, the hoops on necks, the attenuation of some figures may illustrate the contractions of muscles, the dilation of veins, increased heart beat, the sense of weightlessness. Bleeding, represented very simply by two long parallel lines extending down from the face, and sweating, represented by similar lines and flecks flowing from the armpits, more clearly suggest the release

178 *A small section of the paintings in a large cave. Among the images are three elephants by different hands. Two have arrows lodged in them. A hunter is holding arrows of potency below the largest. A beautifully painted group of sable in two colours and showing their white facial stripes has been badly defaced by pecking: recent vandalism probably aimed at removing the pigment for medicine. Bindura.*

of body fluids which some San today recognise as particularly potent in themselves, as the most powerful curative agents or as potency itself. Lines painted up the body or left unpainted within the body may illustrate the 'inner channels of the body' up which active potency is still believed to rise and be released. Incomplete figures are best interpreted at present as illustrating commonly held San beliefs that the body of someone in trance, a trancer whose spirit is absent from his body, is in a sense incomplete.

More striking, dramatic, important and even more closely linked to the activation or generation of potency are the rare figures with grossly distended abdomens, which seem to be direct illustrations of what San believe happens when human potency is activated. The organs of the lower abdomen, the seat of potency, the *gebesi*, swell as potency 'boils'. The release of this potency is represented by lines emerging from between the legs or from the genitalia of some of these figures. These lines are particularly elaborately and carefully delineated, often in several colours. Some twist, meander or change direction in abrupt right angles. One starts along a geometric path such as this but is transformed into a creature with a snake's body and adopts its characteristic writhing progress. Most often they form a careful zig-zag, often extending for considerable distances across a panel. Some are known to end in a few strong, straight, separate hairs that are characteristic of an elephant's tail.

I have established that, in the paintings of Zimbabwe, both in numbers, size, detail and elaboration, the most important image and key symbol is the oval design. It probably had its formal origin in attempts to represent the seat of potency, the *gebesi*. The ovals then represent the internal organs of the lower abdomen, such as the spleen and liver, which some San believe to be the particular seat of potency. Some allusion to this remains in the basic shapes of the ovals, the nesting of ovals of various shapes and sizes within an enclosing membrane, the shapes of the orifices in these membranes, the flexibility of the shapes of the cores and their lack of any skeletal structure or armature. But these allusions to a physical reality are now residual and remote. Aesthetic and conceptual elaborations of the natural prototype overlie it. Many more important allusions derived from thought and belief hide the design's origins, are more compelling and carry much more force. The grandest of these designs seems to have an infinity of caps in the palest shades of paint, massed, piled and receding into an infinity of forms, suggesting the unending extension of potency and the potent community through the universe. In a single image like this, artists recreate visually the immense strength and power of the San concept of the essence of all supernatural energies. In the face of such an image and in the face of the great

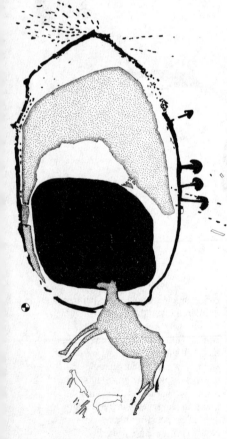

179 *An oval design from which trees grow and flecks flow. Matobo.*

diversity of linked imagery based on the same essential design, it is clear that we are experiencing and dealing with San realisations of their ideas about their most central beliefs, their impressive attempts to depict the non-visible world in paint, to give material expression to the immaterial.

Ovals appear to hold animals between their cores. Animals surmount them. Spirit figures crawl towards them and gather strength as they approach and hold them. They sit on their cusps and peer between and over their caps. Some cores nest like plant bulbs or kernels at the centre of multiple lines that encase them like husks and sprout out at one end like a growing plant. Trees grow from the circle surrounding ovals. Whole panels of paintings may be superimposed on oval designs. Some are groups, like mothers and their children, by a single artist. Others are the most disparate range of images. As these images spread across the rock face, so more and more ovals were added round the periphery of the original design to provide a growing context, setting and field of force for the imagery.

Flecks or dots are the simplest of images but one of the most important. They are so simple that it could well be judged that they represent a great many different things, palpable and impalpable, from bees to entoptics. More detailed consideration of their associations shows this is not the case. They have a coherence, a single basic system of repeated associations that shows that they all are manifes-

180 *A juxtaposition of an oval design, a small field of flecks that may emerge from it, and two figures, one of them recumbent, who seem to dip arrows of potency in the flecks. Matobo.*

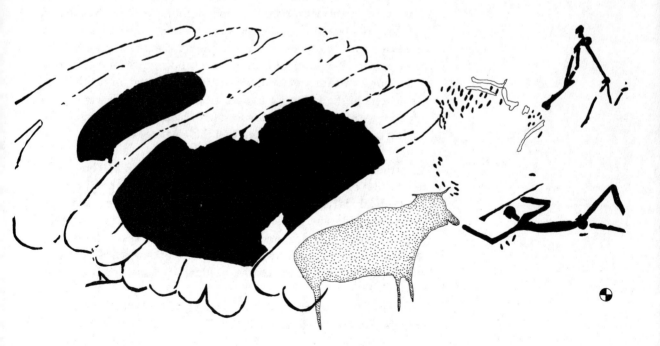

tations of one basic idea, a single San perception of their world. Their visual source lies in the ordered grids of dots painted on the cores of the more complex ovals and is a conclusive visual demonstration of their association with ideas about potency. They frequently flow out of oval designs. They can form tight clusters, often quite small, sometimes very large and sometimes enclosed in a circle. They form large ill-defined fields around very different images. They appear to flow in lines and streams across even greater distances than the lines coming from distended figures. They can be so carefully arranged to take the characteristic shape of an oval with both its core and cap that their identification with oval designs in the minds of the artists cannot be in doubt. They can cohere to form ladder-like forms. They adhere to branched forms to appear as their leaves. They also cluster along the outlines of creatures with animal-like bodies. They are painted over and around hunting scenes and scenes of spirit figures fighting. They flow from receptacles held by human figures.

Above all they are associated with trees and branched forms, with the world of plants and nature. And in at least one painting we can recognise that they act on natural plant forms to transform them in part into oval designs. They do not, however, illustrate subjects found in nature, be it birds, bees or locusts, nor do they represent leaves, grass, rivers, lakes, marshes or rain. Detailed comparative analyses of the full range of their forms, arrangements, associations and origins demonstrate this conclusively.

As dangerous animals are hunted and shot full of arrows, flecks flow from their wounds and from internal bleeding. Blood and potency are once more represented identically. And in known San practice, a trancer's blood, lost in the haemorrhaging of trance, is the most powerful and potent healing agent. But trance is death: not a metaphor for death, not similar to death, but a form of death itself. Depictions of the killing of the most dangerous beasts were given added force by their deliberate defiance of reality, in the imagining of the impossible. The new tensions that this cleavage induced took the imagery into a new realm.

So the paintings of hunts are more than metaphor. They are a representation of a perception of San reality. The power of trance, of trance-death, is the power of the largest, fiercest, strongest and most dangerous of beasts. The elephant is the trancer, the trancer is the elephant. Within this common framework, minor distinctions were made between elephant, rhino and buffalo and perhaps lion. Our interpretations are still too coarse to understand the significances of these.

While all the imagery has a basis in the visible world, some images seem in part creations or inventions of the artist's imagination; they are rather reflections of beliefs in various forms of supernatural beings held by his society. Some conflate otherwise disparate images. These conflations seem to have been at least in part intended to explain some of the concepts underlying the imagery; certainly they do this for us. From our point of view, the most important conflation is that of oval designs and elephants. Caps of closely juxtaposed vertical ovals form a cusped line. This can serve as an abbreviation, reference or metonym for the designs as a whole. This cusped line is then sometimes used to form the backs of some elephants. Other elephants are surmounted by several such lines. This suggests that the concepts embodied in oval designs and elephants are compatible and congruent, that both have similar references, that the one is in some sense and to some degree equivalent to the other. My interpretation that both refer to aspects of potency is thus reinforced. This view is further supported where a large outline painting of an elephant is superimposed on an oval design and thus in some sense is able to replace it, a similarity of usage that is also apparent when it is recognised that the elephant's legs can be unnaturally extended to embrace new images in growing panels of images just as ovals can be added to original compositions to provide an increased field for new paintings.

A very similar conflation is repeated in many images in the Matopo Hills in which the cusped line forms the backs of creatures with kudu heads, snakes' bodies and, often, a gaping mouth. It also recurs in a single group of two-legged trunked creatures at the other end of the country.

Another conflation combines elements of humans with those of birds. In some cases only the legs are recognisably human. All have the outstretched wings of a bird. Many are deliberately grotesque in many ways. Such winged semi-human creatures do not seem to refer directly to any aspect of potency but to illustrate a process of transformation from human to bird. Known San beliefs describe how trancers are able, through activating a particular aspect of their potency, to take on the forms of birds. They do this particularly when, disembodied of their human forms, they seek to travel impossible distances instantaneously, in a quest for other communities or other hunting grounds.

One small conflated image, centre right in fig. 181, is so far unique and was perhaps genuinely idiosyncratic. It was found long after my analyses had been formulated and brings together several elements in mutual reinforcement and provides, it seems to me, the most encouraging visual confirmation of the validity of my analyses. The figure, a man, stands erect with the abdomen of a grossly distended figure, pierced with many arrows characteristic of elephant hunts, with the emblem of tusks of transformation sticking out from his protruding face. Most striking and idiosyncratic of all, he is the sole figure in the paintings known to me that has the careful, detailed and unmistakable tail of an elephant attached to his buttocks. No other image thus conflates three different references to elephants and their hunting with distension of the abdomen. A most important metaphorical image is conflated with the key illustrative image of active potency and a common emblem with a final personal elucidation in the addition of the tail. Only through an understanding of the presence of an overriding concept of potency in its many and varied visual aspects can this image make any conceptual sense. Any other approach to it reduces it to meaningless nonsense. And it is very clear that the paintings of Zimbabwe are not nonsensical.

A few figures appear entirely human except for their heads which have the ears, horns and muzzles of specific species of antelope. They are otherwise so ordinary, and in terms of this particular art system, 'realistic', that they can be taken to illustrate people who have fixed the heads, or at least the skin and appendages, of actual animals to their own. This cannot, however, be taken as a form of hunting disguise or camouflage for the figures never carry any weapons. They may be associated with dancing and with particular dances associated with specific animal species, an extension of those dances in which participants paint their bodies to reproduce the markings of particular antelope.

Different again are creatures with human bodies, antelope ears, generally those of a kudu, and elongated and sharply pointed muzzles, unlike the faces of any other creatures in the paintings. Their bodies and particularly their limbs are reduced to an almost skeletal structure of bone with no flesh or muscle, making them seem weightless. Yet their movements are animated, dramatic and very human and they have many ordinary human appurtenances like sticks and capes. The penises of the men are not only often shown but can have the emblem of a bar across them. Others have the variation on this emblem in which a tufted line emerges directly from the area of the navel. They have relationships with the prime symbols of potency. Some sit on the cusps formed by the caps of ovals, others crawl towards ovals and seem to gather strength from them. Some are surrounded by flecks. Some watch the organised control of flecks. After they were painted, some were surrounded and intertwined with the lines coming from a woman with a distended abdomen.

These are not people in any ordinary sense nor are they creatures of the visible world. They do not correspond to any known descriptions of trance experiences. They are not illustrations of hallucinations. Nor are they idiosyncratic inventions of individual artists because their

characteristic features are reproduced sufficiently often and are so similar that they must illustrate a creature in which all the San communities to which the artists belonged had a firm common belief, both detailed and explicit. Yet their details do not correspond with any known San beliefs. To consider them as spirits of the dead, whom the San believed retained a great deal of their human characteristics, seems the most satisfactory interpretation of them. If this is so then, like beliefs in the supernatural power especially inherent in the elephant, they are another instance of how the paintings can extend our knowledge of San beliefs far beyond the reach of ethnography and with a considerable degree of certainty.

Other images with strong human references may of course represent not spirits but gods. It seems more reasonable at this stage to consider the distended figures as humans whose potency is boiling and swelling in their abdomens rather than as gods. However, the array of emblems characteristically associated with them – head tufts

181 *The most interesting of these images is the man (striped, lower right) with tusks, arrows piercing his distended abdomen and an elephant's tail. Makoni.*

and manes, leaves, combs and crescents – suggests such an array of different aspects of potency that it renders them god-like in the concentration of different powers. Indeed, the gods are believed by the San to be imbued with a concentration of potency far beyond that of any human trancer.

It could be taken that figures with only one arm and one leg should be interpreted in a similar way. Against this is their association with the lines emerging from distended figures. This shows that they are a variant on the distinct category of semi-human figures who crawl towards and clamber up and down these lines but more often cling to them, hang down from them or float above them. Their forms are generally and characteristically fuzzy, shadowy and without clear shape. Where they are clearly detailed and even adorned with strings of beads, they have only one leg and one arm and their heads may be unnaturally twisted. These creatures have none of the diagnostic features of those we have called spirits or of other types of incomplete figures. They belong to a separate category: one suggesting dependence, an as yet incomplete or lost humanity, one in the process of generation or, much less likely, dissolution, seeking fulfilment, impalpable and unstable.

We are constantly drawn back to visual explorations of potency. It could well be that different concepts or forms of potency are represented in the paintings. One may be primarily represented by oval designs, another by flecks, another by multiple zig-zag lines. On another level, one may be represented by recumbent trancers and another by distended figures. One may be associated with the hunting and death of animals and hence have a primary influence on hunting and another act primarily on trees and plants. Put in another way, one may influence the human world, another the animal world and another the plant world. In yet another way, one can suggest that one is primarily concerned with natural fertility, another with animal increase or hunting success and a third with human generation, birth, death and rebirth. Yet the paintings make it clear that the artists did not consider these as separate categories. Ovals have a close association with flecks and seem often to be their source. The same is true of distended figures and zig-zag lines, though in at least one instance the lines have their source in a recumbent trancer. Ovals are added to trancers and can be closely identified with them. Malformed figures, primarily identified with zig-zag lines, are also associated and dependent on flecks and can also be superimposed on and juxtaposed with ovals.

Though they seem so precise and specific, similar overlaps occur with emblems. Some basic rules are distinguishable but no one emblem can be associated exclusively with any particular set of circumstances. One among a group of hunters engaged in the most ordinary of activities, preparing their bows, may hold a leaf shape. A very ordinary little figure with no clear associations can hold large and detailed combs. All we can say at the moment is that an increase in the numbers of emblems attached to people correlates very broadly with situations in which the actions of potency are more important and likely.

Perhaps further work will clarify such puzzles as these and render interpretations more precise. But it is quite probable it will not. The ways San are known to think about, discuss, describe, explore and explain their beliefs about potency and all supernatural phenomena are quite unlike the methods we are used to. Their beliefs have none of the coherence, clarity or precision that have developed in Western thought. They have no dogma, seek no definitions, create no distinctions or boundaries, demand no consensus, accepting apparent anomalies and contradictions. Belief is a lived experience, one open to individual exploration, personal expression and debate. Submissive wonder is more important than analysis. Different names are used for different dances and types of trancer but their definition seems impossible; they seem all very largely interchangeable. And so it seems to be with their paintings. Here once again, beneath the apparent confusion of detail, is visual confirmation of the fundamental San ethos, of San perceptions of life in all its complexities.

In this book I have attempted to analyse various types of paintings and aspects of the paintings consecutively, in a certain order. I have been conscious throughout that this is an ordering imposed by me and that any such sequential analysis has a certain falsity. One experiences the whole of a panel of paintings or any complex visual composition near simultaneously. The rock paintings in particular have no focus of attention like the Western compositions we are so used to, hence there is no set order in which one must view the elements of a painted panel. Indeed, as one tries to analyse the array of images, one feels somewhat like a juggler attempting to keep a great many oranges or plates in the air at the same time. As they pass rapidly through the vision of the scanning eye, one tries to sustain and make sense of their pattern as a whole. If one focuses on any one of them, on any one type or set of images, one is constantly aware that inattention to others is likely to bring the whole act to a disastrous conclusion.

Fortunately the simile is not apt. The paintings are not like the juggler's oranges; each is not distinct and separate, to be caught and held separately. Rather each subject, each set of images, is much more comparable to the atoms or nuclei of a molecule, even the tightly

182 *The disparate and seemingly unrelated palimpsest of images in this small and typical panel of paintings includes swaying, crouching, squatting and recumbent figures; and kudu, tsessebe, unidentifiable antelope and buffalo. Marondera.*

183 *An unusually detailed and realistic painting of a flying raptor, probably an eagle. Two long lines stream from it and an ethereal semi-human figure crouches above them. Matobo.*

intertwined and convoluted spiral of a DNA molecule. Each element is inextricably related to all the others, held together by invisible charges or bonds. So it is with the paintings, once it is recognised that however disjointed they may seem, they are also held together by an invisible force, to form a single coherent system and whole. Significance lies in the charge, in the relationships that bind the images together. There is a unifying and simplifying force that gives all paintings a single shared significance. The juggler can relax. No orange can fall, no plate will shatter; all are interconnected, kept together in the air by a single sustaining force. There is no juggler at all; that which sustains them is invisible and external. It existed in the minds of the artists and not in the visible arrangements of compositions.

The invisible charge that gives the art of Zimbabwe its inner cohesion and structure lies in the apparently universal San concept of an inner spiritual energy, force or potency inherent in different forms in all things, gods, spirits, living people, animals, plants and many forms of matter, even in actions. It gives them the power to attain the supernatural. In many different ways it animates the paintings and gives them added significance. It does not do this through the magical properties of pigments, media or images. These may or may not have been recognised; it is now impossible to know. But it is clear that this is not a necessary premise to understand or recognise the

184 *The outline of an elephant, facing left, has been painted over to supersede an equally large painting of a buffalo, facing right. Along their shared back are crouched malformed figures. The elephant's legs have been extended to cover as many images in the panel as possible. The antelope are tsessebe cows and calves. Marondera.*

185 *A grotesque hunter is shot at and pierced with arrows: a painting from the same rock face as fig. 181. Makoni.*

references to potency. It was achieved because the paintings, through illustration, signs, emblems, metaphors and symbols referred to concepts of potency, and celebrated its presence and power through a sophisticated and rationally constructed conceptual imagery.

It is also not to suggest that the paintings in Zimbabwe are concerned exclusively or even predominantly with potency; they very clearly are not. They do not have a single focus or motivation. They explore every aspect of the society that created them, every aspect of human behaviour. What I do propose is the recognition that the perceptions of, beliefs in and imagery of potency in the world gave the paintings an added dimension, a further level, a heightened significance. The paintings of Zimbabwe do not simply 'lift the veil on the spirit world'. They do not illustrate the supernatural world exclusively or even to any great extent. In any case, in San perceptions the natural and supernatural were not separate realms or distinct spheres, but formed a single unity; the one permeated every aspect of the other. References to the invisible, metaphysical or supernatural pervade the art but the art remains rooted in, focused on and concerned with daily life, not as a record of how it was lived but in idealised, abstracted and generalised statements of its value, its economic, social, moral and spiritual worth. The art therefore was not, as is said to be the case in South Africa, primarily or even predominantly concerned with trancing, trancers or 'shamanism'. These were important aspects of all San belief and practice and the paintings in Zimbabwe reflect this. But it was not of disproportionate concern. The art was in no way bounded, esoteric, or limited in its concerns, in its practice or in people's understanding of it. Like San society it was open, transparent, understood and participated in, practised and legible to all. Paintings range from those that evidence the most refined conceptual mastery, others that are clearly the work of the most able and delicate craftsmen, others that delight in aesthetics and beauty, others that show acute and penetrating observation, some that are simple and earthy down to the most hesitant sketches of beginners. Its conventions, construction and vocabulary encouraged this great range of possibilities. In every aspect of the art we can be sure that we are in the presence of an artistic tradition that, in a highly developed and sophisticated way, brought significance to a now vanished society. It is time to explore it further.

References

1 Hughes, R. 1993, *Culture of Complaint* (New York: Oxford University Press), 187; Ravenhill, P. 1992, *African Arts*, 25, 4: 20.

2 Marshall. L. 1957, 'N/ow', *Africa*, 27 (3), 232–40; 1962, 'Kung Religious Beliefs', *Africa*, 32 (3), 221–51; 1969, 'The Medicine Dance of the Kung Bushmen', *Africa*, 39 (4), 347–81; 1976, *The Kung of Nyae Nyae* (Cambridge: Harvard University Press); Lee, R.B. 1984, *The Dobe Kung* (New York: Holt, Rinehart and Winston); Katz, R. 1982, *Boiling Energy: Community Healing among the Kalahari Kung* (Cambridge: Harvard University Press).

3 Lewis-Williams, J.D. 1981, *Believing and Seeing: Symbolic Meanings in Southern San Rock Paintings* (London: Academic Press); 1983, *The Rock Art of Southern Africa* (Cambridge: Cambridge University Press); 1990, *Discovering Southern African Rock Art* (Cape Town: David Philip).

4 Garlake, P.S. 1987, *The Painted Caves: an Introduction to the Prehistoric Art of Zimbabwe* (Harare: Modus Publications).

5 Garlake, P.S. 1992, *Rock Paintings in Zimbabwe*. Thesis submitted for the degree of Ph.D. in Art History to the School of Oriental and African Studies of the University of London.

6 Walker, N.J. 1987, 'The Dating of Zimbabwean Rock Art', *Rock Art Research*, 4 (2), 137–48.

7 Burkitt, M. 1928, *South Africa's Past in Stone and Paint* (Cambridge: Cambridge University Press).

8 Frobenius, L. 1931, *Madsimu Dsangara* (Berlin: Atlantis Verlag).

9 Goodall, E. 1959, 'The Rock Paintings of Mashonaland' in Summers, R., ed. *Prehistoric Rock Art of the Federation of Rhodesia and Nyasaland* (Salisbury: National Publications Trust).

10 The most relevant example is: Breuil, H. 1966, *Southern Rhodesia: the*

District of Fort Victoria and Other Sites: Rock Paintings of Southern Africa Vol.V (Clairvaux: Singer-Polignac Foundation).

11 Fry, R. 1910, 'The Art of the Bushmen'. Reprinted in Fry, 1940, *Vision and Design* (Harmondsworth: Pelican Books).

12 Cooke, C.K. 1969, *Rock Art of Southern Africa* (Cape Town: Books of Africa).

13 Vinnicombe, P. 1976, *People of the Eland* (Pietermaritzburg: Natal University Press); Lewis-Williams, J.D. 1981, 1983, 1990, (see *n*. 3). Lewis-Williams, J.D. and Dowson, T.A. 1989, *Images of Power* (Johannesburg: Southern Book Publishers).

14 Lewis-Williams, J.D. and Loubser, J.H.N. 1986, 'Deceptive Appearances: A Critique of Southern African Rock Art Studies' in Wendorf, F. and Close, A.E., eds., *Advances in World Archaeology*, 5 (New York: Academic Press), 253–88.

15 Lewis-Williams, J.D. 1972, 'The Syntax and Function of the Giants Castle Rock Paintings', *S. Afr. Archaeol. Bull.*, 27 (105), 49–65; 1974, 'Superpositioning in a Sample of Rock Paintings from the Barkly East District', *S. Afr. Archaeol. Bull.*, 29 (115), 93–103.

16 Lewis-Williams, J.D. 1980, 'Ethnography and Iconography: Aspects of Southern San Thought and Art', *Man*, 15, 467–82; 1981, (see *n*. 3).

17 Lewis-Williams, J.D. 1984, 'Ideological Continuities in Prehistoric Southern Africa: The Evidence of Rock Art' in Schrire, C. ed. *Past and Present in Hunter Gatherer Studies* (New York: Academic Press), 225–52; 1987, 'Beyond Style and Portrait: A Comparison of Tanzanian and Southern African Rock Art' in Vossen, R. and Keuthmann, K., eds., *Contemporary Studies on Khoisan, Part 2; Quellen zur Khoisan-Forschung 5.2* (Hamburg: Helmut Buske), 93–139.

18 Wilmsen, E.N. 1987, 'Of Paintings and Painters in Terms of Zhuhoasi Interpretations' in Vossen, R. and Keuthmann, K., eds., *Contemporary Studies on Khoisan, Part 2; Quellen zur Khoisan-Forschung 5.2* (Hamburg: Helmut Buske), 347–72.

19 Lewis-Williams, J.D. and Dowson, T.A. 1989, *Images of Power* (Johannesburg: Southern Book Publishers).

20 Lewis-Williams, J.D. and Dowson, T.A. 1988, 'The Signs of All Times: Entoptic Phenomena in Upper Palaeolithic Art', *Curr. Anthr.*, 29 (3), 201–45.

21 Lewis-Williams J.D. 1986, 'The Last Testament of the Southern San', *S. Afr. Archaeol. Bull.*, 41 (143), 10–11.

22 Lewis-Williams, J.D. and Dowson, T.A. 1990, 'Through the Veil: San Rock Paintings and the Rock Face', *S. Afr. Archaeol. Bull.*, 45 (151), 5–16.

23 Katz, R. 1982; Marshall, L. 1969, (see *n*. 2).

24 Lewis-Williams, J.D. 1981, 44, (see *n*. 3).

25 Katz, R. 1982; Marshall, L. 1962, (see *n*. 2).

26 Marshall, L. 1957, (see *n*. 2).

27 Marshall, L. 1962, (see *n*. 2).

28 Bleek, D.F. 1931–6, 'Beliefs and Customs of the Xam Bushmen' *Bantu Stud.*, 5–10; Lee, R.B. 1984; Marshall, L. 1962, 1976, (see *n.* 2).

29 Bleek, D.F. 1931–6, (see *n.* 28).

30 Lewis-Williams, J.D. 1981, chapters 4–8 (see *n.* 3).

Index